# Cambridge Elements ≡

**Elements in Histories of Emotions and the Senses**
edited by
Jan Plamper
*University of Limerick*

# ACADEMIC EMOTIONS

## *Feeling the Institution*

### Katie Barclay
*University of Adelaide*

CAMBRIDGE
UNIVERSITY PRESS

# CAMBRIDGE
## UNIVERSITY PRESS

University Printing House, Cambridge CB2 8BS, United Kingdom

One Liberty Plaza, 20th Floor, New York, NY 10006, USA

477 Williamstown Road, Port Melbourne, VIC 3207, Australia

314–321, 3rd Floor, Plot 3, Splendor Forum, Jasola District Centre,
New Delhi – 110025, India

103 Penang Road, #05–06/07, Visioncrest Commercial, Singapore 238467

Cambridge University Press is part of the University of Cambridge.

It furthers the University's mission by disseminating knowledge in the pursuit of
education, learning, and research at the highest international levels of excellence.

www.cambridge.org
Information on this title: www.cambridge.org/9781108964944
DOI: 10.1017/9781108990707

First published 2021

*A catalogue record for this publication is available from the British Library.*

ISBN 978-1-108-96494-4 Paperback
ISSN 2632-1068 (online)
ISSN 2632-105X (print)

# Academic Emotions

## Feeling the Institution

Elements in Histories of Emotions and the Senses

DOI: 10.1017/9781108990707
First published online: November 2021

Katie Barclay
*University of Adelaide*

**Author for correspondence:** Katie Barclay, katie.barclay@adelaide.edu.au

**Abstract:** The university is an institution that disciplines the academic self. As such it produces both a particular emotional culture and, at times, the emotional suffering of those who find such disciplinary practices discomforting. Drawing on a rich array of writing about the modern academy by contemporary academics, this Element explores the emotional dynamics of the academy as a disciplining institution, the production of the academic self and the role of emotion in negotiating power in the ivory tower. Using methodologies from the history of emotion, it seeks to further our understanding of the relationship between the institution, emotion and the self.

**Keywords:** emotions, academia, universities, complaint, scholars

ISBNs: 9781108964944 (PB), 9781108990707 (OC)
ISSNs: 2632-1068 (online), 2632-105X (print)

# Contents

# 1 Introduction

Like so many things, this Element has changed because of COVID-19. When I began researching this topic – inspired in important ways by my own experience of working in the academy – the importance of emotion to the production of working culture in the neo-liberal university was at the forefront of my mind. So it was with some surprise that, in March 2021, as a colleague and I reflected back on a year of retracted sector income, mass layoffs, political hostility from national governments and outpourings of anger and grief from those who experienced these events viscerally, I found myself saying that if the sword fell and my job was removed I was not sure that I would care. A statement of bravado – a hardening of heart in preparation for possible pain? A remark of privilege – the confidence of one that doesn't really believe it would ever happen to her? Exhaustion? All of the above? Even as I said it, I wondered what it meant. Is it possible to be unemotional in the modern university? And what does it mean for an institutional crisis to lead its staff to such a hardening – an emotional closure that implies a vulnerability, or caring, that pre-existed this shift?

That workplaces have emotional cultures is now a recognised phenomenon, often tied to issues of workplace productivity, well-being and success. Toxic workplaces are (sometimes) bad for business. Business management theorists encourage employers to shape workplace emotional culture through encouraging shared values, reducing poor work practices (such as overwork) and by modelling the affective behaviours that they wish to maximise in their environments (Barside and Gibson, 2007). Within some workplaces, especially those which are customer fronting, the expectation that people perform particular emotions as part of their job has been described as a form of 'emotional labour', yet even where emotions are not formally mandated as part of a role, workplaces typically have implicit, often unacknowledged, rules around emotional expression and behaviour that direct how people feel and how they display such feeling while at work (Hochschild, 2012; Bloch, 2002). What that might look like can vary enormously across workplaces, occupations and cultures, and has differential effects. Some workplaces laud overt emotional expression; others supress such feelings; more typically, employers expect a more nuanced emotional range that reflects the dynamics, needs and personalities of particular environments. These different emotional expectations can impact individuals in a myriad of ways; some flourish, while others experience such contexts as harmful.

Workplace emotional cultures are often described as delicate, easily disturbed by a growth in staffing, a poorly behaved manager or a changing employment context (Barside and O'Neill, 2016). Yet, many workplaces are also institutions, sometimes of significant longevity. Within such contexts, emotions are often far from transitory but embedded within structures and practices that have long histories and are part of the make-up of the institution (Rosenwein, 2015). To change the feeling rules of an institution is therefore to ask it to reconsider its nature and purpose, the mechanisms of power that such feeling rules enable, and very often requires its staff to think about their emotional selves in new ways. This is, not least, the case for institutions attached to professions, such as law, medicine or academia, where the emotional culture of the institution typically extends beyond a single employer and is closely tied to the concept of vocation (Barclay, 2019a; Arnold-Forster and Schotland, 2021).

Within such institutions, the socialisation practices of the workplace extend beyond being successful or productive employees to a deeply rooted occupational identity, marked by particular characteristics of which the experience and performance of emotion is one (Moisander et al., 2016; Archer, 2008). In such contexts, the distinction between occupational and individual emotional performances can be especially blurred, and simultaneously more fraught, for those who find vocational emotional cultures harder to access and practise. Emotion workers in customer service roles often recognise a 'front' and 'back' of house distinction in emotional performance, where the polite restraint and civility offered during customer service is discarded for moments of release, such as through foul language, complaining or carnivalesque behaviours (Hochschild, 2012). The collapsing of professional and personal identity within vocational contexts often denies such a distinction, marking failures in emotional cultures as transgressive (Weber, 1919). To change the emotional culture of a vocation is significantly more challenging than tweaking the disorders of an out of sync group of employees; it requires a commitment by the institution and all its members to become something different.

This is not to say that this is impossible. Indeed, as I explore in this Element, one of the key transformations of the academy as it has moved into what is now described as its neo-liberal form has been that such a demand has been made of the university worker, and that this has been far from a painless, or indeed, complete process. This Element explores how the modern academic is institutionalised, and the way that shapes the emotional culture of the university. Partially a reflection on my own university career, it perhaps most tightly captures the experience of a generation of academics who graduated from their PhDs in the first decade of the new millennium and who have been socialised into a workplace where the impacts of various forms of austerity, metricisation, professionalisation and precarity have become increasingly pronounced. However, just as these impacts have not been distinctive of this group, so too has the academy as a body had to move in various ways to accommodate these changes and their attendant emotions. This was perhaps especially the case in 2020, when the retraction of the sector had impacts on staff at all levels, and led to a much wider range of voices entering the public debate around the nature and feeling of living in our current institutions. Yet, if the discomforts of the academy are shared, I would suggest that different biographies – different modes of socialisation while in early career, different levels of seniority as one lived through these shifts, different types of social, economic and cultural capital – have shaped how the experience of being institutionalised in the modern academy feels.

Drawing on personal experience and observation, professional trade writings on the modern academy, academic literature and surveys, Twitter and other social media, this work emerges from an observation of the anglophone academy, particularly in the UK, Australia and the USA. It focuses especially on the emotions of academics, not the larger body of university workers, acknowledging that universities often combine quite different emotional regimes for different parts of its workforce, and that there is not space here to do justice to this diversity. Given the globalising structures of academia, and the movements of academics across national contexts, what is described here will hopefully have wider resonance (Cannizzo and Osbaldiston, 2019). However, I acknowledge that the prominence of anglophone writings flattens some significant complexity produced by national funding structures, cultural values and positioning within an imperial global hierarchy. Even within the anglophone world differences emerge; tenure in the USA has offered some significant protections against metricisation in ways that have not been the case elsewhere, but it has also heightened disparities across groups within the academy – the haves and the have nots. Teasing out the impacts of these various social, economic and national contexts on academic emotional cultures will no doubt complicate any patterns described here.

The purpose of this Element is to consider how the emotional culture of the modern university is produced, attending to the socialisation practices that ready individuals for entry into this culture, the institutional disciplinary structures that uphold these systems of feeling and how such emotion becomes implicated in the production of power. Importantly, the emotional culture of the modern university is far from a naïve effect, but a highly politicised domain, where expressions of suffering are also claims to structural wrong-doing and moments of pleasure and happiness point to the hope of the institution and the reasons for its continuation, despite such suffering. Within this framework, the emotions of the individual are situated as the bellwether of the ethical health of the institution – the ethical crisis they signal often directly informed by the embodied subject whose complaint is registered. Within this context, a booming scholarship on the emotions of universities as organisations – by academics – is simultaneously an attempt at their political reform, as, of course, is this Element. When one no longer feels for (a politically orientated *for*) the academy, a new form of ethical crisis is signalled, one whose repercussions extend beyond the individual to the future of the institution.

## Emotions in the Contemporary University

The university is subject to a substantial body of research covering its history; organisational structures and practices; culture and environment; and possibilities for how it will be shaped in the future (Barcan, 2016; Berg and Seeber, 2016; Bulaitis, 2020; Cantwell and Kauppinen, 2014; Collini, 2017; Connell, 2019; Duryea and Williams, 2000; Ehrenberg, 2004; Fitzpatrick, 2019; Forsyth, 2014; Hrabowski, Rous and Henderson, 2019; Perraton, 2014). A key theme since the late 1990s has been the rise of 'managerialism' in universities, a model that has been driven by an increased demand for accountability, especially over the expenditure of public funds, quality assurance in teaching and a retraction in state funding and push to privatisation that has moved universities to commercialise (Broucker and De Wit, 2015; Reale, Bleiklie and Ferlie, 2009; Shepherd, 2017). Managerialism in universities is typically marked by an increasing divide between management and academic work, often coupled with greater regulation of labour by managers, and so a shifting of the balance of power within institutions (Fabricant and Brier, 2016; Hall, 2018). It is closely tied to the rising use of data analytics to measure staff achievement and growing role specialisation where people are hired to perform particular tasks – administration, teaching, research – rather than the use of well-rounded generalist academics and support administrators (Hazelkorn, 2015; Gannon, 2018; Orr and Orr, 2016).

The growing use of managerialism is also a reflection of universities' exponential expansion, with academic faculties only a small component of big businesses that now include, among other things, specialist services for students (including health care, counselling, academic skills support and careers advice), marketing and fundraising departments, buildings and asset management teams and limited private companies that are fully or partially owned by institutions (Berman, 2012; Cantwell and Kauppinen, 2014). Many components of universities are therefore beyond the scope of academic working life and often operate independently of academic faculties, although the goal of such activities is largely to fund core missions in teaching and research. In the last decade or so, especially in the context of austerity economic policies in much of the west, managerialist practices have been ramped up as part of strategies to increase competitiveness in what is now a global market for students and research funds. As a part of an industry strategy to distinguish institutions in this market, 'independent' ranking systems have emerged that claim to measure quality using a variety of reputational surveys and data analytical modelling, and which are used to market institutions to particular income streams, especially high-fee paying international students (Hazelkorn, 2015). As private income streams have become more significant to university budgets (and this affects different institutions at different levels), the productivity measures used to assess academic staff are largely directed to enhancing scores in the rankings, and this in turn has shaped resourcing across subject areas and individuals in the institution.

These changes to the university are rarely viewed positively by academics, including many academic managers. As much of the academic literature on universities is written by this group, there are very few wholehearted defences of managerialism. For many, it is a necessary evil, for others, an unnecessary one. However defence of individual managerial practices has been more mixed. The use of metrics to measure quality and success in creative industries has been the subject of critique by theorists since the nineteenth century and such arguments have been readily applied to academic systems; yet many defenders have argued that they are better for equity, helping those with less cultural power in institutions, or institutions with less cultural capital, to make a case for their research (Wilsdon, 2015).[1] Specialisation in the workplace has similarly been met with mixed reviews. While some bemoan the loss of the research–teaching nexus that is at the heart of how the academy has often been imagined, others argue that allowing individuals to pursue their strengths offers value to both workers and institutions (Bennett, Roberts and Ananthram, 2017).

In practice, any benefits such practices might enable have been offset by some significant perversities that these systems have encouraged, especially as pressure on budgets increases. Specialisation of role, for example, has been coupled with an economic revaluation of tasks. High-profile researchers, especially those that shape positioning in rankings or government quality assurance activities, are highly valued and often paid well. Teaching is increasingly de-specialised, viewed as something that can be done by junior academics. Significantly, teaching is becoming a casualised task, so that academics are only employed to cover particular courses or on an hourly-paid basis (Kezar,

---

[1] While this has benefited individuals, the benefits for women and minorities have not emerged in practice (Teelken, Taminiau and Rosenmöller, 2021).

DePaola and Scott, 2019; Schuster and Finkelstein, 2006; Tolley, 2018). Such roles provide no support for research, and indeed largely expect the worker to come fully equipped and qualified for the role with limited support for preparation. As many of these workers aspire to full-time academic jobs, they are required to maintain their research outputs without economic support. Many research roles, by contrast, often funded by limited-time funds, are fixed-term contracts, including a significant component of the research workforce at every level (even those of very senior research 'stars'). As these workers are required to continually look for work, there is pressure on them to perform to the metrics desired by university ranking systems – publishing and pursuing research income. This pressure has significantly expanded workloads, workplace stress and unethical research practices (Erickson, Walker and Hanna, 2020; Fetherston et al., 2020; Oakley, 2010). Universities are reluctant to address these issues, as committing to ongoing contracts for workers (many of whom are employed for their distinctive specialisms) is viewed as an economic risk, while a competitive research culture is seen to enhance the success of the institution. This employment context shapes the experience of working for the university and is often framed as being part of the neo-liberal academy, where the structural conditions of labour relations are recognised as significant in the production of the academic self – a self that has long been recognised as embodied and emotional (Taylor and Lahad, 2018; Hall, 2018; Archer, 2008b).

The scholarship on emotions in university life is heavily indebted to feminists who have explored women's position in the university (e.g. Bellas, 1999; Bartos and Ives, 2019). Early research on universities as organisations emphasised the gendered labours of care asked of women in the university, often offset against a masculine culture of competition and aggression. Emotion in such research was typically recognised as a product of working conditions, but less attention was given to theorising the nature of such feeling itself. The 'emotional turn' of the last decade or so has transformed the field, leading to an explosion of publications in the last five years. Feminists remain prominent in this work. Sara Ahmed (2010, 2012, 2019, 2021) has highlighted how analysing emotions as a form of cultural politics draws attention to the exclusion of marginal groups within the academy, and transforms complaint into a political act. Many have built on these observations, particularly attending to the emotional experience of practices associated with neo-liberal workplaces, including metrification, where people's value and worth is collapsed into productivity measures and rankings, and precarity, where long-term precarious employment heightens anxiety and acts to wear on the self (Asdit et al., 2015; Barcan, 2016; Burton, 2018; Cannizzo, 2018; Crimmins, 2018; Haddow and Hammarfelt, 2019; Berg, Huijbens and Larsen, 2016). Significant to this debate is recognition that emotions are a product of structural conditions – the neo-liberal workplace produces a particular type of self with a particular emotional repertoire (Askins and Blazek, 2017). For most critics of the university, neo-liberalism has been associated with an increase in suffering among university workers.

Not all research has been so negative. A number of scholars have sought to chart the joys of academic life, pleasures that are seen to emerge from the core work of institutions – the creativity of writing, the intellectual joys of research, the pleasures of working with and mentoring students (Riddle, Harmes and Danaher, 2017). Some ethnographic studies have attended to everyday emotions, seeking to chart the ups and downs of daily life and so to avoid reductive relationships between tasks and feelings (Bloch, 2012; Ehn and Orvar, 2007). There is also an associated body of work on student emotions and how these emotions shape learning and teacher–student relationships (Pelch, 2018; Zembylas and Schutz, 2016). Interestingly, however, few works have considered the ways that neo-liberal structures might enhance the positive dimensions of academic life. Either such analyses are not located within a framework that attends to the structural conditions of emotional life, or the joys of the academy are situated as moments of resistance to larger neo-liberal systems. At times, finding pleasure becomes a radical or transformative act within a system designed for suffering (Bright, 2017). For others, academic joys are evidence of the way the system 'should be' and are often framed against a 'golden age' of academic life, an era that likely did not exist but which is upheld as an ideal account of the vocation (Archer, 2008a).[2]

This Element contributes to this scholarship on the emotional life of the modern academy, but seeks to bring the insights of a historian of emotion for whom feeling is never simply a response to structural conditions but an active component in their production and in the operation of power. Here, my work is perhaps most indebted to that of Sara Ahmed's reflections on academic life, but I wish to extend her insights to a discussion of how academics are institutionalised to feel and what difference that makes. Within this Element, the academic literature on emotions in the university is therefore both a scholarship that this work engages with and a body of empirical evidence that can be analysed as part of the production of the modern university. Discourse about the university is not removed from its production, but plays a significant role in shaping how academics understand the conditions of their workplace and the appropriate – and inappropriate – responses to its operation. Following Barbara Rosenwein (2006), I argue these academic writings evidence and enable the 'emotional

---

[2] A similar claim is made within the profession of medicine which has followed similar trends to the academy (Arnold-Forster and Schotland, 2021).

community' of the academy, by providing it with a shared emotional language and system of valuation for such feeling.

## Emotional Politics

A key idea in this Element is that the performance of emotion is a political act. Performance here does not suggest that a person's emotional experience is not 'real' to them, or that its expression is inauthentic. Rather, it recognises that emotions are social and cultural products; the naming of embodied experience gives feeling definition, directs how we respond to such feeling and, when communicated to others, shapes their response. To name a feeling 'anger', for example, might lead us to violence, and this embodied performance of emotion might in turn be condemned or praised by others, depending on whether such behaviour is viewed as appropriate. Each of these steps are informed by cultural norms (Barclay, 2019a; Scheer, 2012). What we call our feelings and how we respond to emotion varies and can be affected by expectations attached to our gender, race, age and similar identity markers. How we emote is also influenced by our environments. Different places, whether the home, the workplace, the football field and so forth, have different emotional rules that shape acceptable and unacceptable expressions of emotion in them. As Hochschild (2012) and others have demonstrated, these emotional rules are sometimes explicitly taught, such as by an employer to staff, before becoming naturalised behaviours; at other times, they are encouraged through socialisation practices (Frevert, 2014). Individuals can be more or less successful at learning, and especially naturalising, these emotional rules, and the consequences of this can vary.

At times, a system of emotional rules can amount to an 'emotional regime', where the regulation of the expression of feeling acts to empower or limit those who more or less successfully conform to those rules; here, successful performance of emotion becomes implicated in the production of power (Reddy, 2001). Emotional regimes can be looser or stricter, with some offering more diversity of emotional expression than others. Failure to conform to a repressive emotional regime can cause emotional and other forms of suffering. Within the workplace, failure to conform to emotional rules might limit opportunity to progress, cause conflict with colleagues and supervisors or simply make it challenging to find a 'place' within an organisation (Rafaeli and Worline, 2001). These emotional disturbances, in turn, might have repercussions for productivity or workplace culture. They might also be necessary to producing new workplace cultures that are open to a more diverse workforce – such as when 'macho' organisations adapt to allow the entry of women – or where workplace culture is interfering with the evolution of an organisation into a different form (Currie, Thiele and Harris, 2002).

Emotions in this context are political because they do important work in expressing and shaping the identity of workplaces, in enabling or limiting access and success to different groups of workers, and because the decisions around which emotions are acceptable are fundamentally political choices that act as a form of discipline on the self (Ahmed, 2004; Hochschild, 2012; Gregory and Singh, 2018). Emotions can also be deployed strategically to effect change to environments. Feminists who wished to make space for women in combative academic environments in the late twentieth century often promoted and performed gentler, kinder behaviours as a political challenge to the norm (David, 2016). In some fields of research, this could be very effective, taken up by male allies who recognised the importance of inclusive cultures. Expressions of suffering have often encouraged others to effect change, acting as claims to wrongdoing and a demand for redress. Shared emotional cultures can also provide sustenance and belonging that empower people to act or to mobilise for change (Lipton, 2019b). Emotions are deployed in all of these ways in academic environments and can be both naturalised behaviours and used strategically.

In the modern academy, emotion is also political because it is understood to be a product of the neo-liberal structures that shape the academy and so speaks to the ethics of that system (Evans and Nixon, 2015). Elsewhere, I have explored an 'emotional ethic' as a set of embodied feeling practices that are underpinned by a set of moral principles (Barclay, 2021). I would suggest emotion operates similarly for the modern academy, where expression of feeling acts as evidence of an ethical self and where comfort within unethical conditions is suggestive of a complicity in an immoral institution. This immediately raises the question of whose emotion we are measuring and how that relates to daily life in the university. This is made more complex by attending to the academy as a vocation practised across the globe and by people whose daily working lives can vary enormously – incorporating humanists and scientists, lab technicians and casual tutors, 'superstar' researchers and teaching-only fellows, breathtakingly wealthy vice chancellors and adjuncts who supplement their income with state welfare. Can we posit a group that is so large and diverse as a single emotional community?

The source base for this study reflects my training as a historian, who typically works with the dead and accesses emotion through the texts left by emotional actors, and where such texts are recognised as part of the production of emotional experience. A key issue for this project and one that I return to at the end of this Element is that discussions of feeling in the academy have largely been produced by those for whom it is discomforting – women, ethnic and racial minorities, the working class, early career researchers and the precarious – or those who study these groups. Much of this work has placed such expression of emotion in the public sphere because this feeling is understood as evidence of the dysfunctions of a workplace that is either insufficiently inclusive or exploitative and so harmful to these groups. Emotions here are deployed as complaint and to demand change (Ahmed, 2018). Interestingly, however, research that has sought to offer a more rounded picture of the emotional experience of the university has largely conformed to these accounts (Bloch, 2012; Riddles, Harmes and Danaher, 2017). The privileged white men of the academy, who are often situated as the 'norm' whose comfort is a product of an emotional culture designed for them, do not appear much happier when asked about their feelings (Heffernan and Bosetti, 2021; Ylijoki, 2020). The pressures of the academy are variously experienced across bodies but are largely felt by all.

We might here suggest that happy people are quiet people and 2020 has suggested that this is certainly part of the story – pandemic conditions have destabilised the academy in ways that have radicalised a large number of people for whom working conditions had not been so poor that they felt the need to express such feeling in the public domain. Yet, the other side of this picture is that there is little evidence of that comfort in the source material. One explanation for this is that the literature of emotion in the academy not only acts as evidence of academic feeling, but are key texts in producing the academy's rules of feeling – the modern academy is an uncomfortable place and its feeling rules shape how that discomfort is experienced and expressed. Moreover, it also reflects that the modern academy, discussed in these terms, is not simply a conversation about an individual workplace, especially at a departmental level where there are many more descriptions of positive experiences; rather, the academy is envisioned in terms of the vocation and where local injustices are placed as traces of larger systemic problems. This is not to suggest that the suffering that emerges in the literature is simply a product of rhetorical effect – the ubiquity of shared experiences of injustice and the emotions that arise highlight the realities of these claims for individuals. But it reflects that the emotions of the academy are naturalised across groups as a vocational account of what it is to feel in the modern academy, and where individual feeling – feeling that can highlight the very different levels of power that exist across the academy – is interpreted and expressed using these terms.

This Element explores how this emotional regime is created. It begins by looking at the systems – the training process – through which academics are socialised in this emotional regime, before considering some of the key features of modern academic life. These include the expectation of mobility and the possibility of finding 'place' in the contemporary university; the role of metri-cisation practices in disciplining the academic self; the space for the 'authentic self' – marked by creativity and joy – in the academic labour of teaching and research; and, finally, critiques of the university as an exclusionary institution, reinforcing traditional hierarchies of power. I argue that the academic is pro-duced as a passionate self, whose authenticity is expressed through an articula-tion of the pleasures and pains of the institution, and where such feeling acts as a commentary of the ethics of the academy itself. I have concentrated on argument over descriptions of the rich evidence that underpins these claims and have tried to use examples that arise more from the everyday and mundane than from the tragic. This is partly because an Element is a short work and there is not space to do justice to the evidence, but it is also because I am uncomfort-able with a politics that arises from mobilising the suffering of individuals, and where change is only necessary to counter pain. I would, instead, argue for an ethics that emerges from what we wish to be. To offset concerns about the evidentiary base, however, I have provided significant references to accounts of academic life so that readers can access scholarly emotions as they are practised in word and flesh; I encourage those who wish to know more to engage with these.

## 2 Being Institutionalised

Emotion has long been associated with the life of the mind, and so the embodi-ment of a particular emotional repertoire is part of the successful performance of the academic. The strong link between genius and melancholy for early mod-erns gave the illness a certain glamour for men who desired to be thought scholarly (Vila, 2018). The mid-twentieth-century 'cool' of the rational and objective (largely male) academic was often tied to repressed desires, whether the jealousies that lay beneath collegial relationships or attraction towards the students placed in their care (Showalter, 2005). Such representations remain as part of the academic imaginary of what the academy might have been, but feel increasingly unfamiliar when compared to everyday life in the institution – perhaps especially for those of us too young to have met many such 'characters' during our own careers. Rather, the emotional culture of the university today both draws on this historical memory of the academic self and reflects the disciplinary apparatus of the contemporary university. This section explores how academics are socialised – institutionalised – into the emotional regime of the academy.

Here we are especially indebted to Foucault (1988) whose account of the governmentality of the modern institution has been remarkably influential both for scholarship and for how scholars conceive their own selves. The institution enacts a discipline through its processes, procedures and discourses that shapes and constrains the self; the individual can resist these processes as well as bring their own creative tools to their formation – a continual negotiation that produces the individual within a particular environment. Emotion was central to this process for Foucault, who saw 'passion' as the fundamental feeling that refused systems of governmentality and so offered a place of pleasure (Zembylas, 2007). In this, he was not alone, with various forms of emotion located as the essential self for many mid-twentieth-century theorists, drawing and reframing a long European history of the passions. Emotion theorists have largely rejected this model of feeling, relying as it does on what Rosenwein (2006) has called a hydraulic model according to which people use culture to manage emotions that would otherwise burst forth. Yet, this framework is prominent in many accounts of academic feeling. Academic passion, associated with our intrinsic humanity and its liberties, underlies the ethical claims that such emotion is predicated to symbolise – good institutions should not constrain the possibilities of a pleasure that is the fullest expression of the self.

Important to this model of emotion is that our feelings are our 'authentic' selves and so should be given space for expression (Archer, 2008a; Cannizzo, 2018). Repressing feeling – something that we might consider a routine expect-ation in many professions (Hochschild, 2012) – is considered a restraint on the self, and so associated with suffering. As a result, academic environments often operate on a heightened emotional register; one professional staff member at an Australian university observed that they had never worked in an environment that was so 'emotional'. This emotionality can present itself in multiple con-texts, from the aggressive peer review that takes perceived poor scholarship as a personal insult, to how recipients both personalise and complain about such reviews, to the dynamics at question and answer sessions at conferences and to engagements between colleagues in corridors and meetings.[3] This is not to suggest that the emotional repertoire expressed in these contexts are identical across situations – indeed, there is significant disciplinary and regional variation around the norms of acceptable communication and what might or might not cause upset. But there is a shared agreement that these encounters are emotional and that breaches of the emotional rules – being too aggressive, too angry or, conversely, too sensitive – cause harm.

---

[3] An interesting example of this is the debate over whether people should give 'comments' rather than 'questions' at conferences, where a behaviour that can occasionally be annoying has become a meme and the subject of significant debate over whether or not it is ethical behaviour. See for example: Aswathi on Twitter, 30 May 2021; Scully on Twitter, 3 June 2021.

It might seem counter-intuitive to suggest that an emotional culture that views breaches of emotional rules as significant harms to the individual and the group is overly 'emotional'. Emotional management to this degree is typically associated with constraint of feeling. Yet, what is at stake in such accounts is not the expression of feeling, but how that feeling culture should be performed by its members. Debates over peer review might be suggestive here.[4] Reviewer 2 – the name given to the reviewer of academic papers whose comments are considered especially harsh or as responsible for a paper's rejection by an academic journal – is a central figure in conversations about appropriate academic behaviour, both an academic bogeyman and a meme. Reviewer 2 is associated with emotional behaviours that are seen to underpin their academic critiques, including grumpiness, bitterness, jealousy, aggressiveness and competition. Most significantly, their reviews are both unhelpful – in not helping the researcher advance their work – and diminishing of self. The victim of reviewer 2 feels upset and that upset takes a specific form. A first response is often anger or frustration, followed by a rejection of the feedback and a putting away of both the review and the associated paper. Some people experience significant 'imposter syndrome' at this point, where they doubt their capacity as an academic or ability to succeed in the academic system. A bad review can sour the relationship between a researcher and a particular piece of research. Responses to reviewer 2 can also contribute to larger pathologies, such as depression, anxiety or general mental ill-health. The emotions people feel in response to reviewer 2 are often framed as 'shameful', things that people should not discuss, and the expression of such emotion in public – say on Twitter or a Facebook forum – is an enactment of vulnerability and authenticity to other researchers (Di Leo, 2006).

If such emotion is performed as an expression of vulnerability – and there is no reason to doubt that such feeling is challenging to discuss for individuals – it is common, and therefore contributes to the production of reviewer 2 as a mythological figure and to a well-established body of advice designed to help individuals manage these feelings and to remove the suffering reviewer 2 causes. Advice on this topic operates in multiple directions – there is a body of work dedicated to not being reviewer 2 and to researchers in managing their responses to such feedback (Brown, 2015). Reviewer 2s are encouraged to ensure that they have made an attempt, in good faith, to understand and engage with another's work, and then to provide feedback in a kind form, where 'kindness' is often located as a political action (e.g. Baglini and Parsons, 2020). Kindly feedback usually includes incorporating discussion of strengths

---

[4] A search on Twitter for #reviewer2 can be helpful.

as well as weaknesses, using 'depersonalising' language, for example, replacing 'your argument' with 'the paper's argument', giving specific recommendations for improvement, and being written by someone in the 'right' frame of mind, that is, by someone who is not grumpy! The researcher, in turn, is advised to put aside the reviews for a day or two to calm down and especially not to send an angry email in haste to the editor, which holds the risk of damaging professional networks (e.g. Kara, 2017). They are reassured that such feedback is normal and not a reflection of their general academic ability or the legitimacy of their place in the academy; here, implicitly, researchers are taught to direct their anger at an anonymous bogeyman, who the system has failed to banish, rather than themselves. As a result, reviewer 2 becomes a symbol of a cruel, perhaps even unjust, system and not simply a badly behaved individual, and the researcher is given prescriptive guidance in how to feel and manage feeling in this context.

Reviewers who wish to be viewed as ethical, in turn, experience anxiety around whether they might fall into the category of reviewer 2, and here one of the key tensions of this emotional regime emerges. One of the central pieces of advice given to researchers for managing reviews is to put them aside for a short time and to return to them once the initial anger at the feedback has passed. Often at this point, researchers find that the feedback is not as terrible as originally thought; in some cases, they even find it helpful in improving their scholarship. Thus, the encounter with reviewer 2 is also positioned as a personal emotional journey and not necessarily about bad behaviour by an external reviewer. At other times, of course, the review may indeed be objectively harmful, not least as peer reviewers are the gatekeepers of the academy. Reviewers express significant anxiety around how to express critical feedback, but while there is lots of advice on how to write reviews in kinder ways, it is rarely suggested that a peer reviewer should not give a full report of the weaknesses of a paper. Although there is an ongoing conversation about the value of the peer review system and how it might be improved, as the authoritative truth claims of the academy rest on this system they do not allow kindness to be placed ahead of an honest review. As a result, people continue to give critical feedback that they recognise will be experienced as 'negative', but they can now also ritually perform penance for this in public forums where, rather than being condemned, they are often comforted by other academics who recognise the challenge and necessity of being reviewer 2.

Peer review is therefore located as a place of emotional discomfort and conflict, which needs to be highly regulated to allow authentic expression of feeling and ideas by reviewers while limiting the negative impacts of such expression on researchers. Notably, there is no expectation across any of this discussion that an absence of emotion is possible or desirable, that researchers should not take this personally. The academic is produced in such discourse as an emotional subject whose identity is bound up in their research, so that attacks on their research are therefore felt in personal terms, and that is as true for the writer of a review as the researcher. Critical to ethical action for researchers is not a refusal of emotion, but an attempt to reduce the discomforts of a system where pain is largely viewed as inevitable; however, and perhaps to an increasing extent, the academic is encouraged to take ownership of such feeling as part of academic identity, performing the vulnerable emotive body for others. Importantly, this vulnerable self is not restricted to the research domain but frames encounters with the many other dimensions of academic life.

Not least, academic passion is often inscribed at an institutional level. Senior academics at the University of Adelaide, for example, are asked to write to the selection criteria, 'Passionate and unequivocal commitment to excellence in research and education',[5] while Australian Catholic University offer a 'Passion for the Law' pathway in their Law programme.[6] Scholars also offer 'passion' as a research mode; Ann Game and Andrew Metcalfe (1996) offered *Passionate Sociology* as a model for practice in the field. Such uses of the word passion share in the same imaginary of what the ideal academic is and should be, acknowledging such emotion as critical to an institutional identity where academics are centred. Yet, unlike passion that arises from the practice of academia (explored in more detail in Section 5), such proscription at an institutional level often falls flat and is resisted. Passion should arise beyond the governmentality of the institution – in resistance to it. Trying to institutionalise such feeling is ineffective, as it lacks the 'authenticity' and 'freedom' of the academic passionate ideal. As a result, the failure of university mission statements, brand campaigns and similar corporate messaging to engage academic staff often less reflects the absence of a shared language, than that academic (emotional) freedom refuses such instrumentality. That institutions deploy it, I suspect, reflects that even very senior leaders have difficulty separating their role as 'the institution' from their academic identities; like others, their passion arises from their work for and as part of universities.

That the academic is marked by this form of selfhood might be viewed as a recent phenomenon. As further explored in Section 6, it certainly appears to be the case that the emotional turn of the last twenty years, which in no small part

---

[5] This was evident, for example, in the criteria for the recently adverstised role of Associate Professor/Professor in Psychology. Passion as a 'pointless' job criteria, commonly used by universities, has been subject to critical commentary (Ross, 2021).

[6] See the Australian Catholic University website: www.acu.edu.au/study-at-acu/admission-path ways/choose-your-pathway-or-entry-program/recent-secondary-education/assisted-entry-into-law.

reflects the growing diversity of the academic workforce, has used this vulnerable subjectivity to expand space for different types of bodies in the university
and to express more emotional selves. Yet, many of the stereotypes associated
with anglophone universities in the past – high levels of competition, macho
posturing and collegial sociability – are equally underpinned by this form of
authentic emotional self (Showalter, 2005; Bloch, 2002). The kindness asked of
the modern academic is an attempt to reduce behaviours considered to be
problematic, while still upholding the fundamentals of an academic identity
for whom work is part of the self.

## Training the Academic Self

The academic self that is described here is not a 'natural' self, but rather
a product of academic training. The 'discipline' of a particular field of research
extends beyond methodology to the feelings and behaviours that are required of
the academic. While a proportion of scholars are the children of university
workers and so may have had some familiarity with the emotional rules of the
academy (O'Grady, 2021), most people learn how to be an academic through
the process of research training, and especially the PhD. For the last twenty
years or so, that training has involved combining the vocational with the
professional.

The vocational dimension of academic life is often tied to a long inheritance
of the discipline. New scholars are typically expected to familiarise themselves
with the historical development of methods and ideas in their field, a training
sometimes taught in specific research classes at upper-level undergraduate,
masters or 'comprehensive examinations' at entry to the PhD. They are required
to learn the 'logic' of their discipline, whether the scientific method, close
reading, or what it means to historicise. This education not only provides
students with the general knowledge needed to work in the field, but encourages
them to think of their research within a longer tradition of scholarship and,
importantly, as something produced by a community of scholars. These ideas
are reinforced by academic norms around good scholarship where a 'literature
review' of relevant work is the starting point for new research, and where
inclusion in a discipline requires the scholar to be familiar with a shared
technical language that is often obscure to those outside of the group
(Mewburn and Thomson, 2018). An original contribution to academic work is
explicitly a furtherance of a pre-existing conversation, using its own methods
and terminology. Outsiders can often be identified not because they failed to
understand a particular piece of writing, but because the sorts of questions that
they think arise from such work are not those shared by the field (either because

they've been answered elsewhere or because they don't make sense from its methodological perspective).

This 'discipline' might not immediately be thought of as an emotional training, but a key effect of this project is to inculcate individuals into a specialist and bounded community of fellow researchers. Moreover, and as we will discuss further in Section 5, this is often a pleasurable experience – most researchers choose the PhD due to their underlying, sometimes naïve, passion for a subject (Riddle, Harmes and Danaher, 2017). Time immersed in these ideas is often experienced as fun and personally rewarding, encouraging an identification between the individual and the group producing the work. The bonds of the community are also heightened through what is now referred to as 'networking' – attending seminars, conferences and building relationships with peers, both in person and now online (Ahoba-Sam and Charles, 2019). New researchers are encouraged to engage in these activities for their own well-being – research can be 'lonely' for the sole researcher and research communities offer sustenance and vital support networks (Cantor, 2020). Here, the importance of maintaining mental health, in a context of considerable concern about this issue (Morrish, 2019), is individualised and offered a ready solution. The need for such relationships is even situated as vital to academic success – students who engage with these networks are more likely to finish their degrees than those who do not. Being able to access these communities is therefore considered a key equity issue, underpinning often fraught conversations about how access to these networks can be facilitated for those who are excluded by gender, race, disability or lack of economic capital.

Involvement in academic 'networking' is not simply about strategic career success, but about being part of a community that shares the same passion for their subject, that offers a broad range of forms of support to its members and where many friendships and romantic relationships are born. It is the physical manifestation of the same processes that academics perform when they situate their research within a broader literature review, iteratively reinforcing that the practice of research is also that of community, and so a dimension of the self. One of the consequences of this is that real or perceived exclusion from these communities is interpreted as a failure of the group to offer welcome to newcomers or those who are situated at academia's margins. This politics of inclusion extends beyond access to networks to the politics of citation, where reference to another's scholarship acts as a form of recognition of the self and so affirmation (Smith and Garrett-Scott, 2021). Many individuals take the absence of citations to their work as slights or at least as a failure in the exercise of care in research – a care that is simultaneously considered poor scholarship and a failure to recognise the other. When such absences extend to the exclusion of a particular group – such as women or black researchers – they reinforce the experience of discrimination within the academy and its attendant sufferings.

An external observer might suggest that this picture evidences an unhealthy over-identification with one's work, but in some important ways this misses how academia is not just thought of as a job, but as a community, a vocation and a political commitment. Many people pursue a career in academia because they believe in the importance of their research and its capacity to enact change in the world. The research of the academy actively shapes public policy; underpins legal decision-making; determines community health, welfare and the distribution of resources; and informs cultural norms. Academic research has caused significant harm to some groups, while the academy gives authority to individuals and their ideas. Many people, especially from minority communities, understand access to the academy, and legitimacy within it, as critical to the possibility of social justice for their home communities. As a result, for some an identification with their research is further heightened by a sense of urgent need for social change.

However, even where such personal identifications with the field of research are absent, part of the modern training of the academy produces similar effects in the researcher. Over the last thirty years research funders have prioritised work with 'real world' impact or effects (Smith and Bandola-Gill, 2020; Chubb, Watermeyer and Wakeling, 2017). New researchers are therefore trained to make connections between their research and the political project of improving the world outside the academy. For researchers in fields where these connections are more challenging, this can be a source of considerable frustration. At times, people are encouraged to 'play the game' and to learn the language of impact, without fully embracing it (Burton, 2018; Butler and Spoelstra, 2020). Yet while some are willing to do this, such 'game-play' has further politicised all research and encouraged robust defences of why people's work matters, if not always in the terms rewarded by funders. One of the effects of such rhetoric has been that most researchers now understand their pursuit of knowledge as a political project, which acts to further invest them in their academic identities (Ruben, 2012).

While there are still a few who continue to argue for purposeless research as a value in its own right, such defences are increasingly hard to find, and usually point to unexpected value that might emerge. This is not to say that everyone feels passionate about their own research, and certainly not all of the time (see discussion on sullenwizard, 2020). In a research environment where many scholars work on other's large, funded research grants, the idea of self-directed passion projects is becoming rarer. Yet, when people express doubt about the value of their research, they are encouraged to consider their contribution to the greater good – as the snowflakes that combine in an avalanche – and to the careers that they are building through developing their research profiles, which are predicated on the larger good that is academia. Only rarely is it suggested that it might be acceptable to do mindless, passionless research; indeed, that people display anxiety about feelings of boredom or disconnection from their research is itself suggestive of the emotional expectations placed on researchers. Academics are emotional bodies.

Situated against this vocational training but heightening its effects is a new emphasis on professionalism and career-building. The latter has emerged in response to the growing managerialism of the sector and due to a growth in the numbers of PhDs being produced by universities, recognising that not all these individuals are being trained for the academy. This burgeoning of research training has been resourced through public funds due to recognition that enhanced research skills are needed by the broader economy (OECD, 2012). Yet, even within the academy, professional standards are viewed as a way of increasing efficiency, while providing an evidentiary base for the 'meritocracy' to which many in the academy are committed (Mandler, 2020). As a result, research training now extends beyond the practice of research to consider the full range of activities that might be asked of an academic – teaching, administration, grant capture, organising events, publishing, community engagement, industry partnerships – and to helping people translate the skills they learn for other employment contexts. It is accompanied by an entire industry designed to support academic professionalism, including endless advice on increasing productivity; guides for research – especially writing; software and similar applications designed to enhance efficiency; and blogs, comic books and forums that offer support and induct new researchers into academic culture and norms.[7]

Through this body of work, the researcher comes to understand themselves not only in terms of their relationship to other members of the academic community, but according to conventional markers of academic success, often described as 'lines on a CV'. Partially due to a retraction in resources and, especially, access to permanent jobs, expectations for successful performance have escalated dramatically over the last two decades, intensifying workloads and levels of stress, particularly among early career researchers. Professionalising technologies have often been presented as helpful tools that clarify expectations, make the playing field more transparent for those without cultural capital and allow academics to be more efficient and productive. Yet, as many commentators have observed, they have come with increased

---

[7] A few examples include the work of the Thesis Whisperer, The Professor Is In, Helen Kara, Piled Higher and Deeper, WIASN (facebook) and The Productive Academic (blog); see Lamont, 2009; Brennan, 2020.

expectations and a heightened pace of knowledge production – a pace that for many devalues research by putting productivity ahead of quality and deep thinking.

To return to my argument, professionalisation has not reduced an identification with academia as a vocation, but rather acted as a discipline on the academic body, where new standards of productivity are internalised, pursued and often cause despair as targets continue to grow. The professional academic is now what the ideal academic should look like and self-esteem can be closely tied to achievement according to such measures (Archer, 2008a; Haddow and Hammarfelt, 2019; Brunila and Valero, 2018). Those whose CV does not look sufficiently productive are open to criticism. This can occur within universities as employers deploy performance measures to assess staff, but is also reflected in the anger expressed by many academics who feel excluded from secure jobs in the academy (McKenzie, 2019. The levels of productivity now asked of early career scholars is often measured against career academics whose CVs appear less stellar by the measures that are given emphasis in CV-building (largely publications and grant income) and this disparity contributes to a growing sense of injustice that the academy now relies on work by two groups with very different material conditions – those with 'permanent' jobs and those without.

More commonly, and as explored at length in Section 4, academics often reject the imposition of this disciplinary system while having to live within it in practice, a phenomenon that is often experienced as living in a place of tension, where competing interests continually pull on the self. A desire to meet targets and be successful or to 'game-play' to win grant income competes with the sensation that such a performance is a failure to fight for the underlying value of the research or of a political commitment to the academy as it could be (Fitzmaurice, 2013; Arvaja, 2017). Here, the vocational self and the productive self are situated as oppositional, and academic existence as a struggle for passion and authenticity within an environment that demands compliance. Such a framework reinforces the experience of the academy as one in which emotions bubble beneath the surface and find relief in momentary emotional expression, whether outpourings of complaint on social media, pleasure in research or teaching, or anger expressed towards a colleague when things appear unfair (Fem-Mentee Collective, 2017). While such emotion can be disruptive and sometimes cruel, it is nonetheless valued as an authentic part of the academic persona. The ethical significance of such feeling increasingly comes to be determined by whether it has been targeted appropriately by the affective subject. Emotion, then, is not only an expression of the feeling self but a communicative tool that can produce community or be used to express its boundaries.

## Leaving the Academy

The effectiveness of academic socialisation practices is perhaps most marked when people leave the academy in early career, which is often experienced as a process of grief (Harris on Twitter, 19 May 2021; Barcan, 2019). Today, when beginning a PhD, good supervisors and institutions are encouraged to warn candidates of the challenging job market, where the holy grail of the permanent balanced teaching–research academic job is increasingly rare (Cruz, 2020). Students are only encouraged to continue with further study if they would find pleasure in the process for its own sake, where they see it as a doorway to non-academic career paths or where, despite the odds, their commitment to becoming an academic makes them wish to pursue the career. Many students who seek this advice continue with their plan to do a PhD; this is sometimes viewed as an act of hubris. Yet, I would suggest that for many, especially those for whom the academy was a little-known entity before entry to university, the holy grail academic job does not yet hold the fascination that it does for those within the system. Rather, it is through the process of being socialised to be an academic – a process where the self is actively encouraged to imagine itself as part of an affective community – that such aspirations are born and nurtured.

Once embedded within the academic system, talking about alternatives to academic life can be an emotional minefield. The givers of academic advice are typically not best placed; they are often holders of continuing jobs, whose own messy career paths are not readily visible. Further, and as the label 'alt-ac' (alternative academic) jobs suggests, advice coming from those within the academy tends to situate leaving the institution as a loss or failure, rather than a natural pathway expected of most graduates (Cruz, 2020). In a similar manner, the casual and fixed-term jobs that have proliferated in the academy in recent years are not situated as a 'career', but as a stopover, before one finds an academic job or leaves the institution altogether – a rationale that allows for such roles to be poorly supported or integrated into university life, and so outside of the affective community sought by academics.

The suggestion of alternative careers can be received with frustration by students who are now acculturated into this community, and sometimes perceived as tenured academics closing the door behind them and shutting them off from the resources that sustain the academic self. Working-class and other minority groups who have been routinely discouraged from academic pursuits in early life sometimes view this as a yet another rejection of their ability, tenacity or potential.[8] Acknowledging the unrealistic expectations placed on early career researchers looking for permanent posts – which actively

---

[8] This theme emerges in several chapters in Michell, Wilson and Archer (2015).

discriminate against those with disabilities, caring responsibilities or who need to work – can be interpreted as an endorsement of those same expectations (as can the fact that these expectations still shape hiring decisions). Some emotion is also driven by the relative privilege of many early career academics, whose class background and previous academic success, has ensured that a systematic closure of opportunity has been rare for them. Rather than being received as an ethic of care – which some academics, at least, intend – these messages are heard with resistance and frustration, often refused in favour of practical advice according to which they might heighten their chances of 'winning' the academic game – or at least being allowed to compete in the game.[9]

An increasing number of students now view the PhD as a route to somewhere beyond the academy and make the decision to leave with few regrets or concerns, but for those for whom the academy was an ambition, sometimes a home, making the decision to leave can be especially painful.[10] Some experience this as a personal failure and disappointment, but what is much more likely to be expressed publicly is the feeling of anger at an institution that asks so much of its members before discarding them. This anger can be directed both at systemic problems – the lack of secure employment – and at individuals who benefit from the institution, including other academics and academic services offering advice on how to succeed.[11] For groups that remain structurally excluded from the academy, due to gender, race or other factors, a decision to leave is often accompanied by a strong sense of injustice, not least given the outward claims to merit that pervades academic training. The hurt caused by the academy for those forced to leave is substantial and can shape how they look back on their university experience for many years. Some feel it necessary to cut all ties with academic life, including past friends and research interests, to be able to move forward on another career path.

Academia is sometimes described as a cult, an acknowledgement of its capacity to shape the self and to limit the capacity of individuals to imagine a future beyond it.[12] In recent years, not least as work intensification has

---

[9] The thread at Josh is writing on Twitter, 5 March 2021 – including the quoted tweets by many more senior academics – is productive here as people explore whether the writer's anger is warranted, or whether he is shooting the messenger. This conversation also sparked a number of 'subtweet' conversations, for example, Mittermeier on Twitter, 6 March 2021.

[10] This is articulated in a large body of writing known as 'quitlit' (Shreve, 2018).

[11] This can be seen in the critique of 'academic grifters', who are thought to earn from other's suffering by selling them hope in the form of career advice. For example, the post that appeared after 'The Professor Is In – Karen Kelsky' was described as an academic grifter on Twitter (Kelsky, 2020).

[12] Marinetto (2020) summarises the main interventions in the idea that academia is a cult, but the phrase is now popularly used on Twitter when people feel the academy asks too much of its members.

heightened the demands on the academic worker, there has been a greater push to articulate university work as a job, as something that can be left behind at 5 p.m. (see, for example, Wogrammer, 2012; Roberts-Miller, 2014; Bernier on Twitter, 8 April 2021). Yet, even as many academics would endorse the value of such a mental framework for health and well-being, the emotional training of the academy refuses its logic. A commitment to the academy takes particular forms, including a performance of passion that refuses the confines of a nine-to-five job, and where the absence of such passion is suggestive of one's failure to 'be' academic. Discussions around leaving the academy reinforce the power of this affective community and its passionate commitments, where moving on is vocalised as a loss marked by anger, pain and grief. Such outpourings of pain act as a political protest and challenge to the institution in its current form, while simultaneously affirming that the academic self is one with big feelings expressed loudly to signal our authentic academic identities and ethical commitments.

## 3 Finding Place

The efficacy of the enculturation into academic life provided through research training and the affective networks that support research belies the fact that many people experience entry and inclusion in the academy as a significant challenge. Entrance into the academy requires both technical knowledge and the ability to deploy a shared disciplinary language, as well as certain performative capacities, including confidence in public speaking, asserting one's opinion boldly, a willingness to argue and debate, to think critically and often rapidly and to display mastery of the key issues in a field. These capacities, reflecting the long-standing legacy of rhetorical education in the contemporary academy, are a form of cultural capital particularly associated with middle-class private school education (Minnix, 2018). University culture can also bring expectations around, among other things, appropriate dress and speech forms (including in relation to regional accents and dialect forms), knowledge of and access to certain popular cultures (books read, music listened to, films watched), shared conventional beliefs and similar educational pathways and trajectories (Michell, Wilson and Archer, 2015; Wayne and Yao, 2016; Loughran, 2018; also, discussion arising from Barton on Twitter, 24 March 2021; O'Shea on Twitter, 28 April 2021). It involves being able to express the right emotion, about the right things, in the right context, or at least being able to 'fake' it. Becoming an academic requires a discipline not simply of mind and emotion, but of the body, where one learns – as best one can – to move, display and express oneself as an academic. This section explores how diverse bodies find place in the academy, not least given significant expectations of geographical mobility for researchers and an increasing trend towards precarious contracts.

Because the process of becoming an academic is so closely associated with the production of the authentic self, socialisation within the academy is often experienced as an attempt at balancing 'fitting in' and being received as 'legitimate' and retaining a connection to pre-existing identity cultures, including home and family life. Some groups find this experience easier than others. A key change in recent decades, however, has not only been increasing demands on the institution to open up to new social groups, but growing success in forcing such claims to be heard (Atay, 2017). This was certainly true for women when they entered the academy in significant numbers in the twentieth century, but it has escalated in some important ways, shifting conversations from access to reform. Many people now feel that implicit expectations to change their accents or ways of speaking, to dress in particular styles or conform to particular world views are not only an infringement on the self but a form of discriminatory practice. This can be directly tied to some constructions of academic freedom, where a collapsing of work and self in academic identity leads to personal expression becoming itself a marker of academic freedom.

Individual university cultures, and particularly department-level cultures, can be especially important in setting norms here. Thus, race and gender studies departments are usually (but not always) more self-aware and inclusive on issues of gender, sexuality and race; universities with large working-class communities and staff tend to be more supportive of such groups (Mackinley, 2016). Being trained in such a location can be significant in instilling confidence in non-traditional academic personas that can be maintained as people move across institutions. Studying at the University of Glasgow, with its significant working-class population and many nationalist academics, played no small role in my maintaining a Scottish accent across my career, despite considerable critical commentary as I moved south. In contrast, entering an elite university or conservative department early in a career can encourage significant conformity to academic norms, but also instil a stronger sense that one's place within the academy is legitimate.

The experience of coming to 'fit' within institutional life demands considerable energy, reflected in anxiety and care over self-presentation, the work involved in gently and not so gently re-educating a community to re-consider its standards, and in processing the fallouts from such re-education, whether that is extended personal self-reflection over how a situation was handled or managing escalating conflict (Decuir-Gumby and Williams, 2007; Caruso, 2021).

Microaggressions, the small indignities that question your place within the academy, can result in significant frustration and anger, and contribute to poor mental health and well-being, especially when they mirror larger social injustices experienced beyond the academy (Khoo et al., 2021). In this way, belonging within the university can be refused to some individuals and groups, so that even when they manage to develop a comfortable academic persona – an authentic institutional self – they are nonetheless routinely reminded of their outsider status by others. If finding place is harder for those who sit outside a white, middle-class norm, institutional hierarchies and performance expectations bring their own pressures to appear intelligent, worldly, knowledgeable, productive and so forth. Imposter syndrome can be significant here, but so too can more everyday anxieties about appearing academic enough to others for whom such action appears natural (McMillan, 2016).

Becoming an academic almost always demands some evolution of identity to conform to institutional norms and sometimes it is the changes we embrace that challenge a sense of belonging. New languages and dress codes, new forms of speaking, new ways of thinking about the everyday, new values and expectations for living that enable our academic presentation simultaneously dislocate us from home communities or families. This is often especially remarked on by people who come from cultures that place a low value on education and whose families show significant discomfort with the new knowledges and beliefs held by an individual (Kezar, 2011). Indigenous scholars can find that the logics of western knowledge systems are incompatible and dismissive of their own, and so conformity to such knowledge systems can raise challenges of place (Caruso, 2021; Nakata, 2007). Some people just find that their life experiences become so different from that of their families that they lose shared commonalities and points of interest.

Entry into the academy, then, can be experienced as a loss of family and culture, which, when accompanied by a similar instability of inclusion within the academy, contributes to a feeling of having no natural home. As family or group connections reduce, the significance of the academy to personal identity becomes heightened, not least as friendships, love and other necessary resources of the self tend to be drawn from an academic network of like-minded people. This can heighten the stakes of remaining in the academy, even as opportunities for work and working conditions reduce. Not everyone feels entry into the academy as such a significant demand on the self, but even for those who find an academic identity with greater ease, universities and their environments have internal rules that must be learned by new employees – lessons that must be learned with increasing regularity in the mobile academy.

## Mobility and Movement

For the modern academic – and in many other industries too – mobility is hailed as a social and economic good. A high turnover of research stars, far from signalling a dysfunctional system, is often used as evidence of a competitive research culture. In contrast, the conservative impulses that tighten borders, limit visas and restrict movement are regarded unfavourably, as lacking business sense as well as for their racism. New scholars are not only warned that mobility will likely be vital if they wish to remain with the academy but are sold it as a research good – it will broaden their experiences, produce new research networks, deepen knowledge and understanding (Torralba, 2020; Lau, 2021 – see also the replies to the former article tweeted by Baty on Twitter, 23 May 2021). That the ability to move is a privilege that those bound to place and people cannot achieve is often ignored, as are the academic missions that a familiarity with place might advance (Jamie, 2020; Lund and Tienari, 2019; Ivancheva, Lynch and Keating, 2019). Many of the benefits of moving are realised by individuals. Experience of different academic practices and cultures can expand perspectives, introduce a scholar to new methods and approaches and provide access to different ways of doing the university (Heard, 2018). It is especially useful for expanding research networks that increase international reputation and impact, and building lasting friendships that sustain the self and the research.

At the same time, mobility is a challenge to the ability of individuals to experience belonging within the academy, and especially individual institutions (Cohen et al., 2019; Drążkiewicz, 2021). Moving to a new location entails a risk, not least economic, so that onward movement can be a period of anxiety and excitement. For many, but especially those who arrive alone, a relocation to a new city can be accompanied by profound loneliness and a feeling of disconnection from the safe and familiar (Duffy, 2015; Saunders, 2018; Hancox-Li on Twitter, 13 April 2021; Vatansever, 2020). Finding a place in a new institution by necessity involves a period of unsettling and settling – those moments of trying to find a new routine, learn new faces and the location of buildings on campus, figure out your role in a new set of group dynamics and ultimately build the bonds that enable communities to function (Barclay, 2019b; Ortolano, 2020). Here, the possibilities of comfort in the institution accord with learning its rhythms and understanding how to contribute to their production. Mobility is therefore a process that is underpinned by an experience of being out of place and its attendant anxieties and overthinking, a mental experience that can be likened to the muscle pains of trying a new set of exercises at the gym. Over time, that experience can even be identified – the regular mover comes to know that this process of settling is what is involved in finding 'place'.

Like any bodily labour, mobility also has larger impacts on the self. With every move, the labour of finding place seems harder, the desire to do it again reduces. The longer a person stays in one place the more comfortable it becomes and the more the idea of leaving impacts on general well-being, and on the sense of precarity produced by insecure labour (Berents, 2019; Leo, 2014). Some may say that such comfort produces complacency, but bodies need time to rest and recover. They also need the security that being in 'place' and having community enables – a community that is generally formed through the emotional labour that academics do with those around us when we arrive (Manzi, Ojeda and Hawkins, 2019). At certain points in the life cycle, such stability can be critical – emergency babysitters for the new parent; a carer to bring food or clean the house for those with cancer; knowing doctors that provide support for disability or chronic disease – all relationships that require trust, obligation and time. Thus mobility becomes a remarkable privilege, not accessible to all and with real benefits and pleasures, but also a form of work that contributes to the challenges of negotiating an economy where secure contracts are hard to find and of finding place within a university whose welcome includes a significant discipline of the self.

For highly mobile workforces, and many academic institutions contain as many or more migrants as locals, the mobility of the academy also has implications for institutional cultures. The people met at work are not just colleagues but become family, a support network, a safety net. Mobility dislocates academics from the world outside – making bonds beyond are not impossible but the labour far harder, requiring more effort. At its best, it is a system where family is found at work; at its worst, it reinforces the abuses of the dysfunctional home. Such emotional bonds complicate lines of power, heighten disagreements between colleagues and lead to romantic connections in places where the ethically minded would suggest they should not be. The university often benefits from this process. The pleasures of research often provide succour for the lonely; long hours at work compensate for absent connections in the wider community (Chen, 2018). Friendships that are also academic networks reinforce work as central to identity and promote engagement in academic activities and research culture. Disentangling oneself from work becomes an active commitment to separate from the institution and to find place elsewhere.

## Precarious Mobilities

The impacts of mobility on the self are heightened by a significant reduction in long-term and especially continuing contracts. Many people spend a significant period of time on fixed-term or casual contracts, especially in early career (Adsit, 2015; Ferreira, 2017; Hartung et al., 2017). In some areas, such as the biological sciences where jobs are tied heavily to grant funding, whole careers can be spent on such contracts, with universities offering promotion but not security. Some categories of work, like adjunct teaching in the USA, are also felt to interfere with the possibilities of gaining secure work – there is some evidence that employers for tenure-track roles in the USA prefer new graduates, rather than those with more experience (Patton, 2012). Casual roles, often hourly paid and contracted a semester at a time, can be especially challenging to live on, not least as they often do not provide a financial cushion that might support someone between contracts.

Poverty is a significant issue here in shaping mental well-being – the worry, anxiety and mental effort of trying to survive across multiple contracts, sometimes across many employers, is a significant factor for all workers who live near the poverty line and university workers are not immune from that (Flaherty, 2020). However, even those academics on well-paid fixed-term contracts have increased levels of anxiety and insecurity, underpinned by having to continually search for new work or new funding to support employ-ment. These conditions can be closely associated with overwork as individuals desire to remain 'competitive' in an employer's market.[13] They are especially challenging for people who wish to have children, or who become seriously unwell or disabled – gaps in productivity can be difficult to navigate between fixed-term contracts, something recognised in 'career-restart' funds that largely target female care-givers as a gender equity measure (see, for example, Rogers, 2016). It is a system that is unforgiving of periods of fallow and, indeed, of the rhythms and flows of the life cycle in general. Insecurity is also heightened because of the scale of academic mobility, where many people move countries to remain employed, something that can become more chal-lenging over time, especially for those who have a partner with their own career or children to relocate. The cost of the 'excellence' that is now a standard part of university rhetoric has been the disposability of workers when they fail to maintain it, and that we all live with the knowledge of our disposability and the fragility of the career that is so central to our sense of self (Brunila and Valero, 2018). As Shepperd on Twitter (1 April 2021) comments, 'This generation doesn't so much "become" academics, as much as it survives the business of higher education.'

---

[13] On overwork in academia in general, see the discussion arising from Summerville on Twitter, 24 April 2021.

Living on such contracts can be marked by an odd imbalance of privilege and insecurity.[14] Insecure contracts are held by many top researchers – well-respected and influential thinkers, people with significant power in their fields – but they are nonetheless vulnerable to the insecurity of their contracts and the pressure placed on them to perform at a level that will keep them in similar roles. As seniority and success grows, confidence in finding new work might increase but the losses entailed if required to move to a new employer or country remain. Career is located here as the primary identification for living; we are expected to place it before all else. Academics who are responsible for winning funds to ensure employment for staff on fixed-term contracts can also be impacted by living alongside this insecurity, remarking on the stress that is associated with being responsible for other's livelihoods (Salt, 2002). Some who move on to permanent positions feel survivor guilt, an emotion that is fuelled by growing resentment towards the limited lucky few that get such contracts (Atom44, 2020).

Living within such insecurity can be very hard. Many on fixed contracts report that insecurity acts as a wearing away of the self and mental well-being: 'exhausting', 'humiliating', 'unsettling unease' and 'ashamed' are reoccurring terms (Beudel, 2021; Perera on Twitter, 5 June 2020; and replies, Moss, 2020). Anxious feeling manifests in eye tics, clenched jaws, painful, tense bodies (Liu, 2021; Sinykin, 2016). The self becomes raw, less easily able to manage other harms or criticisms. Within an employment system where failure is routine – whether the unsuccessful grant application, the rejected article or the missed contract – mental well-being becomes hard to maintain, the joy harder to find and responses to ordinary stressors more challenging to manage. After ten years of fixed contracts, I experienced this as hyper-sensitivity, whereby I seemed unable to dampen my reactions to what should have been routine situations. As one academic put it, 'if you've ever been scared of losing your job – it's like that but all the time' (Lister on Twitter, 3 December 2019). If academia promotes feeling as a marker of the authentic self, precarious systems not only heighten such feeling but make it challenging to manage its polite expression.

The emotional disturbances of precarity are marked in an advice industry designed to calm the academic self – yoga, mindfulness, therapists, productivity rituals, all put to the service of finding a sense of control in the uncontrollable (see, for example, Posick, 2018). These are personal solutions to structural harms, offered not only by managers but by academics attempting to survive this system. Recovery takes years. Many people report two to three years before

---

[14] This is a huge topic covered on Twitter by the hashtags: #precarity / #precariat / #precaritystory / #precaritystories, as well as key accounts like: https://twitter.com/acaprecariat; https://twitter.com/PrecariousPlace; https://twitter.com/PrecariousUni; https://twitter.com/PrecariousAcad1.

their anxiety subsides and they start to experience some joy again (Carey on Twitter, 22 April 2021; for replies, see Rees on Twitter, 21 May 2021). Others feel as if they will never recover. I recently celebrated my twentieth wedding anniversary and looked back to find I'd lived in separate homes and countries from my spouse for six years of our marriage *for this career* – information that I don't know what to do with, other than wonder how we can ask that of each other. Precarity is an experience that makes it hard to live within the modern university, not only as one watches as others share similar experiences, but as new performance measurement systems deny any safety or comfort to those who are successful. Safety, in many ways, is one of the critical values of tenure in those countries where it is offered, as important as academic freedom. Many survivors are left with anger and resentment at this system, an emotion that is largely directed towards new managerialism practices or the larger structural conditions of labour, and rarely at the vocation and community that bound them into an affective connection that they did not wish to sever (McKenzie, 2019). This too denies any comfort in the university.

As well as the personal impacts of precarity, the mobility of the system also shapes the relationship between individuals and their universities. Mobile 'superstar' researchers and casual staff alike are no longer bound within systems of loyalty or connection to their employers. Rather, the system, like other neo-liberal workplaces, encourages individualism in all directions. The casual worker should come to the institution fully trained and able to work, offered minimal on-the-job training or support, and be able to prepare resources and teach in a restricted time frame.[15] Employability skills – whether professional development in teaching or the research outputs that make one an attractive hire – are increasingly funded out of pocket – the uberfication of the university. Casual staff marginality is often further heightened by limited institutional integration – casualised academics do not have access to the same resources as other staff. This can create deep ironies where universities, keen to promote teaching excellence, purchase innovative pedagogical tools and programmes or run campaigns around topical issues like academic integrity, which large chunks of their teaching staff are unaware of, and unable to implement. The marginality of casual staff can sometimes be figured literally through their physical place-ment, not even offered desks to work from, perched instead in campus cafes or library hot desks. In Australia and the USA, staff on non-continuing contracts now form the majority of academic staff.

---

[15] This can be seen, for example, in casual teaching rates; although a highly skill workforce is typically required, casual contracts are often relatively low paid or offer minimal preparation time.

If casual staff perhaps epitomise the distance of the employee from the university, such distancing manifests at all levels. The senior researcher should fund their salary and their research through grant applications – money that is often tied only to them and which can move with them if a new employer can promise similar research conditions. Staff employed on such funding are precarious not only to an employer but to the needs of their grant holder. Balanced teaching–research staff must teach enough students to cover their cost to the institution. Workload models, which often significantly underestimate the time required to do a job, are designed in such a way as to encourage staff to prioritise their time efficiently and to focus on those tasks that bring glory and prestige – tasks that typically heighten an individual's reputation as well as an employer's (Kernohan, 2019). The institution becomes a temporary house of mobile entrepreneurs, imagined not in terms of loyalty to an organisation, collegiality or connection to place, but as resources to be exploited for as long as feasible before they move onwards. Here, institutional systems encourage a 'cooling' of the affective dynamics of academia, an act which simultaneously renders universities as unethical (lacking in passion) and incompatible with the vocation.

Except of course, every institution relies on an increasingly small number of permanent academic staff who hold vital institutional knowledge that enables continuity in systems and practices (Huntington on Twitter, 21 May 2021). Research, as well as the affective community that is academia, requires collegiality and camaraderie, manifested in shared research activities, mentorship and a commitment to support each other – a dedication that comes in tasks that go unrecognised and largely unrewarded. Our ethical commitments to our students, and to our sense of professionalism, require us to ignore the logics of workload models to ensure the best possible experience. As importantly, many university leaderships also desire such collegiality, frustrated by a rhetoric of 'us and them' that, especially in recent years, has often manifested in outright hostility between groups on campus (Heffernan and Bosetti, 2021). Universities function better when people find place, but the precarious self – a self destabilised by institutional cultures, high levels of mobility and systems that refuse to offer comfort and safety to staff – acts as a continual challenge to the ideal of the academy. Much of the intensity of feeling around COVID-19 reflects that mass layoffs of staff only intensified underlying fears and anxieties that were latent in staff bodies, as well as spreading such emotion to those who had previously been protected. Expressions of this discomfort, both between colleagues in institutions, directed against managers and as a commentary on the academy more broadly, are placed once more as evidence of the ethical selves of the academy that are undermined by an immoral system.

## 4 Discipline

The term 'the quantified self' was coined in 2007 to describe a movement of people using technologies to measure their performance, whether steps walked, blood pressure or working efficiency (Lupton, 2016). Such technologies are not just associated with the private sphere, but used by employers to set targets and track employee achievement, and by businesses to understand and engage with their markets. Even creative practices are now measured in inputs and outputs, and importantly, impacts (Commonwealth of Australia, 2018). Within the academy, the professional self that is formed through academic training is now maintained through a similar discipline of metrics – counting systems that seek to measure and account for the value of the ineffable – and so are productive of an academic quantified self. This section explores these practices as a form of discipline on the academic self, which produces suffering that contributes to the sense that the institution is unethical.

The metricisation of the academy has operated at multiple levels. National and international ranking systems that compare universities across the globe drive institutional strategies and behaviours (Hazelkorn, 2015). Relationships between staff and students are now measured on a scale through customer satisfaction-style surveys (Phan and Childs, 2017). Citation counts and journal impact factors, both of which are based on counts of references to academic scholarship by other researchers, are used to judge the relative uptake of ideas within the research community (Haddow and Hammarfelt, 2019). Non-citational disciplines, which includes most of the humanities as well as creative works, have sometimes tried to rank work through the reputation of publishers. Counts of research income are often significant. All of these shape academic behaviour and feeling, both as they are internalised as measures that successful people should achieve, and as institutions use them in performance management.

The quantifying siren song, as the Danish philosopher and social critic Søren Kierkegaard (2019/1846) remarked in 1846, is seductive in its seeming production of a level playing field: the ability to measure everyone with the same stick is democratic. Yet, he argued, it came with several losses: first, it promoted unethical behaviour as people sought to work to the system of measurement rather than towards an intrinsic value or good that the system was supposed to measure; and it resulted in a loss of 'subjectivity' or 'passion', a denial of humanity and its ethical basis (here, we can see parallels with Foucault's passionate ungoverned self). The metricisation of universities has been subject to similar criticism. International rankings where weighting is given to grant income, citation counts or 'star' journals, such as *Nature* or *Cell*, are not designed to enquire into the detail of the research that underpins such counting, but rather to use these as evidence of the good things that are going on beneath the surface. Over time, however, these measures became valued in their own right, rather than for what they represent. Far from indicating value, counting practices in the university sector are argued to destroy what is meaningful, reducing world-changing ideas to their uptake in a two-year period, or suggesting that a contribution to French history can somehow be straightforwardly ranked against a laboratory experiment. The idea of the metric as a 'proxy' for something else – something bigger and more valuable – is routinely used in justifications of metricisation systems in universities, even as those proxies have now been mainstreamed as the value that scholars should work towards. As Hannah Arendt noted in *The Human Condition*, as long ago as 1958, contemporary science now works in a world where 'speech has lost its power', having become a 'language of mathematical symbols which, though it was originally meant only as an abbreviation for spoken statements, now contains statements that in no way can be translated back into speech' (Arendt, 1958, p. 4).

For the academic worker, as Arendt suggests, the location of value in numbers forces a narration of self that happens beyond speech. In professional development reviews, grant application narratives and academic CVs, the scholar is encouraged to move from a description of their contribution to the discipline to a count of number of publications, normalised citation factors or income. The academic is no longer expected to articulate their value in terms of their scholarship or its contribution to society, but in comparative measures with other researchers. 'Fairness' is built into this system not through attending to the person and their work, but through 'relative opportunity' where an individual is expected to explain why various career gaps, such as due to maternity or ill-health, account for a lower rate of productivity than might be expected of someone of that career stage. Such comparisons produce a hierarchy between researchers, driving competition and the over-productivity that has marked the academy in recent years – many (especially when starting out) wish to be at the top to gain a competitive edge, not simply to pass a threshold of achievement that 'performance management' might suggest (Lipton, 2019b). The competition this creates sits at odds with the vocational self and its commitment to relationality and community, pitting individuals against those with whom they collaborate and denying the collective effort that is required for knowledge production (Arvaja, 2017; Berg, Huijbens and Larsen, 2016). Importantly, such accounting ignores the individual and their own personal values in relation to their relative positioning and, in doing so, shapes the self in a particular form. The metricised self of the academy is increasingly bland and one-dimensional in being accounted for through numbers, a model that denies access to those who do not easily fit such a mould or whose contribution comes in a different form. Ranking systems that discard those who fall below a certain level of achievement reinforce this uniformity, by removing the scholars and institutions that fail to compete.

Many people experience writing the self in such terms – along with its accompanying vocabulary of 'excellence', 'international', 'top', 'influential' or 'competitive' – as challenging, viewing it as incompatible with the modesty and humility that marks 'polite' discourse, especially for women (see replies to Baty on Twitter, 23 May 2021; Salminen-Karlsson, Wolffram and Almgren, 2018). Some, too, reject the idea that they need to be 'stars', situating their identity in professionalism and quiet competencies; this is especially marked for those who identify more strongly as teachers (see the thread at u/smaller_bear, 2020; Potter, 2021). Producing the self in these terms can be discomforting, while even academic readers can find such accounts boastful, irritating, confrontational and/or demoralising. As significant can be the sense that the self that is composed through numbers is one that fails to capture what many scholars value – ideas, emotions, creativity, curiosity, connection, collaboration – and so is a construction of a self that feels unsatisfactory, empty of what matters to the writer/enumerator. In this sense, the academic self produced through quantification, like the discipline it suggests, is not always a self that is desirable in the eyes of the subject – the tension between the professional/ vocational manifested in the gap between the scholar as a person and their quantified persona. For those whose numbers are viewed as less than excellent, or below expectations, such an accounting can be doubly dislocating, requiring individuals to narrate and identify as a failed academic self, with all the pain, frustration, anger and shame that entails (Horton, 2020; Wolfe and Mayes, 2019).

As these metrics are applied throughout the life course of the career, not least for those who are now performance managed on those terms or who require such success to fund their salaries, quantification practices can continue a precarity often experienced in early career. If some grow in confidence due to the ability to articulate their comparative success, for those whose achievement is less easily measured in such terms or who have simply been less able to attain similar numbers, metricisation can destabilise their sense of security in their employment and, especially for those who have been successful previously, cause considerable distress at the refusal of their status. At times, this can manifest as significant anger and aggression as their positioning is recentred in the academy (O'Neill, 2014; Heffernan and Bosetti, 2021; Jones et al., 2020). With many success measures often closely tied to luck – getting a grant or a high-status publication in a highly competitive industry – metrics can also act as a reminder to everyone of their contingent status in the academy. A spate of 'bad luck' might destroy an academic record and with it the security and self-esteem attached to quantified performances. Awareness of this contingency can contribute to a sense of insecurity for all workers, which is heightened when the academy contracts in size.

This is not to suggest that all academics come to the quantified self, especially particular metrics, with universal disapproval. Many – and this may be a generational issue, more often voiced by those for whom precarity has been less significant – look positively these demands as a *discipline*, ensuring that researchers in permanent employment earn their salaries, or that the research conducted by universities is 'high quality' and good value for money (Wilsdon, 2015; Hazelkorn, 2015; Peseta, Barrie and McLean, 2017). That metrics are at least transparent and universal, not least when contrasted with the inequity produced by 'old boys' networks' and similar systems, has also been recognised. The significance of these numbers for success also allows a good accounting, or an improved ranking, to bring pleasure to individuals. The h-index, a measure of an author's productivity and citation impact, for example, is often noted for bringing happiness, perhaps because while it can stall, it never goes down (Lupton, 2013; Female Science Professor, 2013; Husemann et al., 2017). That the relative value of an h-index is particularly discipline sensitive, so that it is hard to use comparatively beyond the field, may also lead to it as a measure that notes success without providing an easy read of position relative to other scholars. The pleasure of such numbers is built on a sense of achievement, but, at least in part, it also marks that such success offers comfort within a precarious and competitive system. Good numbers, it is at least hoped, will increase the chances of a new contract, permanent employment or the continued rewards that accrue from academic achievement. They bring the recognition of peers, who make assessments of worth based on these terms. Notably, even if people dislike such a quantification of their careers, it is only rarely refused, understood as necessary to the business of academia, and so routinely found on personal biographies, web pages and similar descriptions of career identities.

The value of research metrics to the individual might be especially manifest in the willingness of some to behave unethically or to 'game' their results through their publishing practices (Butler and Spoelstra, 2020). Fudging data or results, or salami-slicing findings (publishing lots of small articles that make similar points from the same study) to enhance their competitiveness are now considered significant issues within the academy. Stealing others' ideas or insisting on authorship for only tangential contributions cause similar concerns (Luther, 2008). While some may be driven to such behaviour through desperation in a precarious academy, others view such action (especially when they do not directly break professional ethics) as part of the logic of the system, and even fun for those who take pleasure in the competition. Game play here, a common metaphor to describe such behaviour, can bring a sense of achievement, but also offers an excuse for why people have instrumentalised their careers towards a systems of metrics they don't value (Butler and Spoelstra, 2020). As one professor noted, 'I was like, "I am never going to, you know, play the game" ... My plan was always to do what I have to do, and then I can subvert once I'm in position [to subvert]. But the amount of subverting I've done is not so much' (quoted in Butler and Spoelstra, 2020). The game becomes an excuse that, once embodied, it is hard to distance oneself from, not least as seniority increasingly does not come with the freedom of action that is often imagined in accounts of 'tenure' or the promise of continuous contracts. Stakes now remain high across the career course.

A result of this is that expressions of happiness or relief around metrical valuations are often rendered with a degree of cynicism, deployed using an agreed and gently ridiculed language of success: 'academia's professionalized feelings – excited – delighted – thrilled', as one Twitter user noted (Snackowski on Twitter, 21 May 2021). People wish to acknowledge their achievement, while holding themselves distant from any suggestion that they have succumbed to the logics of the game itself. In this way, the embrace of quantifiable success measures also becomes a failure to resist or subvert a system that is understood as destroying the fundamental values of the academy. This can lead to the academy as a place of perpetual discomfort, where advancement becomes a further corruption of the ethical self. Ironically, those who refuse to play this game – and who may suffer in their career as a result – can also be subject to criticism and resentment, from those who feel they take up space, especially in permanent jobs, that could be filled by those more willing to do what is needed. Moreover, even the most cynical of game players will often apply such measures when judging the careers of other scholars, seeing this as a critical component of a 'meritocracy' where achievement should be rewarded.

Notably, cynicism towards these metrics is not distinctive of academic staff at the lower levels of the academy, but persists as people rise through management and apply such measures to others. When asked to explain these decisions, blame – a term I use intentionally – is usually pushed further up the ladder and often to the business-orientated university councils for whom such summary data can be used to assess the performance of management teams, to attract international student income or to satisfy the wider expectations of governments and funders who require transparency and accountability of public funds (Hazelkorn, 2015). Few wish to be held accountable for the application of such metrics to workforces, and most reports of them tend to be strewn with warnings about their tendentious nature. Perhaps because of this, many govern-ments have been equally concerned about how such measures have reorientated academic cultures, providing other forms of accountability – such as measuring student satisfaction, impact or commercialisation – to counterbalance more widely used research metrics. There is now a large industry providing surveys and data that can be used to produce new forms of narration of the institutional self, with universities selecting rankings that highlight their particular strengths. Far from building confidence in such measures, however, their proliferation has heightened scepticism around what they measure and which of them should be taken seriously. Despite this, academics and institutions alike persist with their use, unwilling or unable to offer alternative imaginings of accountability – an example of Herzfeld's (1993) 'social production of indifference' where the rituals of bureaucracy provide a barrier to recognising the humanity of those within the institution.

Not all academics wish to be superstars and once in continuing employment attempt to find a personal performance standard that ensures they meet the demands of their institution (and these vary enormously) and their own sense of achievement. The rhetoric of 'publish or perish', however, remains significant to how people evaluate their performance, where 'perish' retains its emotive edge, an existential threat to a self made through the production of research (Rawat and Meena, 2014). While the pleasure produced by teaching – explored in the next section – allows many to reframe their engagement in the academy in relation to other parts of the job, the lack of status that often affords such positions can also impact on personal self-esteem and how they are treated by colleagues or managers (Rawat and Meena, 2014). The result is that the academy increasingly produces itself through a system of evaluation that it does not value, and from which staff and institutions alike hold themselves at a distance, even as its logic shapes their nature. The academy is produced as a divided self, or a self under attack from itself, and so as a fragile institution on the verge of disintegration – a perception of the institution that sits strikingly against another set of numbers – the massive expansion of universities, their incomes and their place within local economies (Ashwin, 2015).

The divided self of the academic, now often tied so closely to neo-liberal metricisation practices, is not unique to the current institution. The lack of passion that is missing from institutional life has been observed across the second half of the twentieth century, but it was earlier tied to a failure of 'objectivity' to offer space for the personal and the human in the production of knowledge. The opening up of research practice to incorporate the qualitative, the subjective, emotion, affect and so forth was driven in some important ways by scholars who felt that objectivity was, to quote A. P. Bochner (1997), 'stifling innovation, discouraging creativity, inhibiting criticism of our own institutional conventions, making it difficult to take risks, and severing academic life from emotional and spiritual life' – a sentence that could easily have been taken from current critiques of new public management of universities. That contemporary metricisation practices are located as external to the academy allows them to more easily rendered as an imposition that can be resisted, but they are also suggestive of the cultural authority of our own scientific disciplinary apparatuses (those we often apply to other groups to improve their efficiency and productivity) and the ways in which they are uncomfortable to live within. Rejecting numbers as a system of academic evaluation forces us to consider the nature of our vocational selves, where numbers, statistics and benchmarking are central to scientific languages and practice. Our cynicism at our own metrified success hides a deeper discomfort with the institution, its work and what it stands for, which repeatedly manifests in critiques of the modern university.

## 5 Creativity and Joy

Set against the insecurity of current working conditions and the disciplinary practices that constrain the self are the pleasures of the job. Teaching students, mentoring colleagues and perhaps, above all, creating research are situated as sites of meaning and passion for the academic. Not everyone enjoys the same parts of the job – some prefer teaching or research – but nonetheless there is shared recognition that these are the dimensions of academic life that mark the value of the university. Finding pleasure in these tasks becomes an act of resistance to a neo-liberal institution that is often imagined as undermining joy, whether that is through the commercialisation of the student–teacher relationship or the intensification of workloads that remove time for exploration and risk-taking. Passion is produced through a self that situates itself as open, experimental, hopeful, creative and feeling (Riddle, Harmes and Danaher, 2017; Singh on Twitter, 10 March 2021; Honan, 2017; Schepelern-Johansen, 2020). This section explores where academics find their passion, and so the passionate self.

Far from the loneliness of the ivory tower, academics today tend to locate well-being in connection with others. Relationships that extend beyond collegiality or friendship to teaching or mentorship are especially valued for the sense of satisfaction and purpose that comes from helping others succeed (Moss et al., 2018; Kern et al., 2014; Lipton, 2019a; Gannon et al., 2019). Moments where students 'get it' or excel are considered particularly joyful, and offset the worry, frustrations and long hours that often accompany teaching. The opportunity to produce meaningful relationships is viewed as significant here, where large class sizes or the black screens of zoom teaching reduce the opportunity for pleasure to emerge. The teacher as content-provider model sits in opposition to how teaching is framed by most academics, as emerging through less tangible connections, shared affections and joint exploration. In contrast, grading for large classes can be considered a slog, if with moments of pleasure in the occasional piece of academic excellence, as can lecturing to a camera with no audience for an online lecture (Bijl, 2020; Melby-Lervåg on Twitter, 4 December 2020). For those who enjoy it however, teaching is rendered as a full and complex human experience, with emotional highs and lows but (hopefully) a sense that such work matters (Sadler, Selkrig and Manathunga, 2017). The dissatisfactions of teaching can be tolerated if they emerge from the unevenness of working with other humans in the classroom or the mundane nature of some of its associated activities, but less so if they are viewed as an external force corrupting the teacher–student relationship or the demands of administrative creep (Lutz on Twitter, 8 May 2018).

The practice of research is often figured as similarly meaningful, with its value emerging in how people feel as they perform such work, as well as its contribution to a 'greater good'. Scientists particularly value the emotions of curiosity and wonder, locating them as emotional drivers of the research process (Chen, 2018; Taylor, 2020). Discovery can even be described as a sublime experience: 'It is almost indescribable . . . what you feel is really something you cannot express with words. It is a profound and incomparable feeling' (Salas, 2018). Humanities and social science scholars can share such feelings – the cry of joy from the historian who finds the perfect source in the archive suggestive of the pleasure of discovery (Reiter, 2015) – but such language does not always capture the emotions of a scholarship that emerges from interviews, thematic analysis or close attention to a text. Scholars here might describe a sense of urgency emerging from an ethical project to which their research contributes, the desire to create the world anew through new narratives or the pleasures of immersion in the experience of the others – to encounter the fullness of humanity (Crimmins, 2017).

Many people identify doing research – the stepping away into the world of intellectual pursuits – as a place of calm or peace, the thing that compensates for the stresses of the workplace or everyday life (Duncan et al., 2015). As such, research can be figured as an 'obsession' or 'addiction' for some; like other addictions at their extreme, some researchers will give up family, partners, friendships and more in the pursuit of their passion (Britton, 2018; Chen, 2018). The pleasures of research soothe loss. Across the academy, the process of exploration is typically valued more than the production of outputs – the writing up of results for a public audience. A popular meme shows a circuit with four boxes: Get new idea>Start new project>Tell everyone>Get new idea. The fourth box – Finish project – sits outside the circuit, acting as a commentary on a seeming flightiness of academic desire. Its popularity however speaks to a community that values the thinking and the doing, as much as the finishing. Exploration, new ideas and formulating new research plans bring their own pleasures, often more significant than those offered by a successful research output (that typically comes with the pains not only of writing, but of peer review). Joy lies in the thinking.

Writing, by contrast, can be a much more mixed experience. Some people love writing; others find it a chore. But regardless of what is felt about the overall process, it is generally regarded as a form of labour with inherent challenges and risks (Bright, 2017; Burton, 2018; Mackinlay, 2016). Academic writing, like all writing, is a conversation, a co-creation of knowledge and contingent. And yet, to write is to make authoritative claims as to the nature of the world – the past, the present, the future – and in important ways to make something real out of a mass of possibility. It also an aesthetic process; people worry about form and the beauty of knowledge's presentation. Thus, writing is accompanied by trepidation, by pain and frustration, as well as moments of joy and pleasure. Writing can be considered 'hard', something to avoid or procrastinate, and is associated with an industry of advice to make it easier or more manageable (see, for example, Carter, Guerin and Aitchison, 2020; Firth, Connell and Freestone 2020; Dunleavy, 2003). Writing also brings anxieties as texts move into the world, first for peer review, and later to a broader audience – anticipation of a text's reception can add to the burden of writing. The final text that closes the experiment (at least in this form) and which then becomes the measure of an individual's academic success or failure, holds a different set of pleasures and pains from the research process itself. Putting a piece of writing into the world becomes an act of vulnerability; revising and editing a text is made easier by 'alienation' from it, pretending it was not your work, as one tweeter suggested (Boddice on Twitter, 22 May 2021). Writing becomes the creation of the research self, one marked by the constraints of the genre, and so also evidence of the successful achievement of disciplinary norms.

As academic research outputs – for example, publications in professional journals – have become central to the politics of success in the academy and so viewed with some suspicion as an instrumental measure of knowledge-making, alternative forms of output have flourished. Some – such as those aimed at non-academic audiences – are given value by their ability to open up the academy to a wider group. Other forms – like exhibitions, art or digital productions – may remain relatively specialist in their audience but seek the possibilities allowed by new representational modes. Perhaps most tellingly, work by academics critiquing the industry often engage with creative forms – poetry, cartoons, drawings, life-writing or rhyme (see several examples in Black and Garvis, 2018; Gill, 2009; Charteris et al., 2016; Gannon and Gonick, 2019; Henderson, Honan and Loch, 2016; Manathunga et al., 2017). Creative writing is situated here as an alternative to traditional academic writing, where the passion of the academic (restrained by the neo-liberal academy) is allowed to emerge. To produce a critique of the academy in its own language seems to defeat its intention – to render dull and boring what should be full of life. If this is the case, such attempts at academic 'freedom' are also subsumed by universities whose democratic expansion – the desire to give the authority of the academy to other knowledge forms – has led to the incorporation of creative industries, as well as other knowledge systems, into its disciplinary regimen (Holeywell, 2009; Myers, 1993).

The joys and pleasures of academic life have been situated by several writers within Lauren Berlant's concept of 'cruel optimism'; our faith that teaching and research have value, bring joy and ultimately give merit to academia as an institution, encourages us to persist within a system that is otherwise cruel and detrimental to our well-being (Lipton, 2017; Thouaille, 2018; Berlant, 2011; Coin, 2018; Osbaldiston, Cannizzo and Mauri, 2019). The pleasures of the academy here are sublimated to neo-liberal structures or to an exclusive conservatism that makes life uncomfortable for many of our members. For others, the joys and pleasures of the academy – not least, when configured as creative writing forms performed in small group workshops of like-minded hopefuls – are moments of resistance, the imagining of an academy as it could be and steps towards a different future (Kern et al., 2014; Mackinlay, 2016). In both accounts, the teaching and research that most universities retain as their central mission, and their associated happy emotions, are secondary to cruel disciplinary structures. That universities might be joyful emotional regimes, occasionally disturbed by overbearing managers or financial insecurity, or even their own culture that sits alongside a neo-liberal structure, is not imagined in most critical accounts of the modern university.

Despite this, a number of surveys show that many academics find happiness within their jobs, if not every dimension of them.[16] For a small elite, happiness is found in their personal academic success and commitment to the institution and situated against the 'complainers' who are located as 'lazy' or unsuccessful,

---

[16] For an example of hundreds of academics discussing their happiness, see the Twitter thread that arose from Ager on Twitter, 5 February 2021.

their claims of suffering considered as unreasonable (Ylijoki, 2020). For some, such happiness is combined with an embrace of metricisation, at least to the extent that the demands of such systems are considered useful evidence of productivity, rather than a system of oppression. Responses to accounts of 'happy academics' are not typically well received, viewed as lacking compassion for others or wanting in political awareness of the realities of the inequities of academic life. To be happy in academia, without a sufficient awareness of the politics of the neo-liberal workplace, is a privilege that is hard to stomach. The moral academic self – that may or may not find pleasure in the job – cannot be happy while the majority suffers.

## 6 Suffering Bodies and the Absent Norm

Accounts of unhappy academics have been described as 'misery narratives', stories where suffering is deployed as an ethical commentary on the wrongs of the contemporary university (Ylijoki, 2020). Happiness too has been a subject of concern, a feeling that being placed as a moral good makes such stories hard for the comfortable to stomach – Sara Ahmed's feminist killjoys whose complaint discomforts, removes the happiness of all and so places the complainant as a troublesome problem (Ahmed, 2010, 2021). Notably, while the pain of working in universities has been expressed by people of all genders, races, employment statuses and levels of seniority, a key feature of much writing on the problems with the contemporary academy has been produced by those whose bodies, desires, social background or beliefs mark them as 'different' from the white, middle-class norm. This has been an incredibly rich scholarship with significant transformational power, now held up by many academics as examples of critical injustices that institutions must address, as well as a cause of considerable friction, simplified and dismissed as 'identity politics' (see, for example, Ahmed, 2012; Attewell, 2016; Black and Garvis, 2018; Brown and Leigh, 2018; Garrod et al., 2017; Matthew, 2016; Pereira, 2017). This section attends to this conversation because of the way it conforms to a model whereby ethics arises from the pleasures and pains of the academic body, and yet is one of the few places where questions have been raised about the usefulness of this form of selfhood.

Bodies matter here. It is not only that certain bodies are marked as different by their inability to conform to the norm – as non-white, non-male, non-able-bodied – and so encounter casual cruelties and aggressions (Matthew, 2016; Brown and Leigh, 2018), but that embodiment plays a significant role in the performance and experience of suffering in the academy. The cruelty of the institution is not simply a denial of the right of entry to particular identity groups, but that the bodies of some groups fail to flourish within structures that are not built for them. Here, attention has especially been drawn to menstruating and bleeding bodies, to breastmilk and leaking milk ducts, body fluids that seep through clothing and destroy performances of 'professionalism', or biologies that produce pain which debilitates, disrupting the capacity to function (Pine, 2018; Bosanquet, 2018; Moss, 2019). The academy is not simply rendered as a place where work extends and interferes with the 'balance' needed to procreate and raise a new generation or to engage in cultural obligations, but where the personal – the grief of child loss or debilitating hormonal responses or the incarceration of your community's children – comes to the workplace and struggles to be incorporated within an industry for whom the private and the public are distinct spheres (Caruso, 2021). Institutions have found ways to compensate (if in limited ways) to bodily events that are discrete, temporary and largely happen outside the place of employment (such as maternity leave), but not for those that are everyday, ongoing or a fundamental part of the self.

The logic of the academy continues to rest on the idea that there can be a separation of work from other dimensions of the embodied self, even as the authentic academic persona is expected to conflate identity with work and to build their self through academic relationships. The institution demands a reformation of the self into the academic, a vocational commitment and professional discipline, and now, for many academics, asks them to leave behind family, attachment to place and natal cultures. And yet, the academics who embrace this and bring their own embodied selves into the academy are resisted by its systems. Metricisation becomes especially unforgiving here in its reduction of academic success not only to narrow parameters but to those that implicitly drive quantity of product as an expression of worth. The value of new perspectives or insights, radical reimaginings or diverse bodies to knowledge production – claims that often figure so clearly in academic scholarship as things that are good and valuable and necessary (see, for example, Tuhiwai Smith, 2013; Collins, 2013; Moreton-Robertson, 2004) – is dismissed by the orientation of the modern university towards rankings that are inherently conservative and which struggle to expand to incorporate diverse bodies and careers.

Rather than rejecting this logic, narratives of suffering, produced by critics of this system, sacrifice the body to the institution. On the one hand, they demand that the institution is refigured as a more inclusive, perhaps compassionate space. Yet, they also offer up the body, its fluids, aches and histories, to the academy as suitable for its discipline – as something that should and can be incorporated into academic life. The body, and often very vulnerable and moving accounts of its suffering, is surrendered to the institution in the hope that it will change. In doing so, such claim-making reinforces an academic persona that is all encompassing, the researcher and the person as a single authentic self, and also configures the academy as something that is worthy of this self, of this vulnerability and humanity. The academy becomes a utopian society made small, where the success of all the groups within its structures is a sign of our capacity to make such changes beyond its doors. The university is no longer a 'workplace', where 'reasonable adjustments' or non-discriminatory practices are the limits of an expectation of inclusivity, but the future that our research should enable. In many respects, this is as it should be – a morally inflected *should*. If new futures are to be built on the research of universities then all communities must be given space in the institution: 'Nothing about us without us'. Yet, offering the body to the university also embraces its empire-building logic, where external knowledges, methods, practices and experiences are increasingly cheerfully embraced but required to conform to its discipline in an anxious hybridity (Lal, 2002; Dear, 2019). The academic is not permitted to hold a self outside of the institution.

Notably, in many accounts of the suffering body in the university, the institution that is produced is that of its community of academics and other staff, and they are held responsible for its failures (Khoo et al., 2021; Matthew, 2016). Racism, sexism, homophobia and other discriminatory or harmful practices are depicted as products of everyday encounters between humans in the academy. If academic emotion is a bellwether of university ethical health, the ethical failure that is signalled by such pain is that of other academics and it requires them to do the self-reflection and personal reform that will allow the academy to change. This is complaint whose target is known, identifiable and uncomfortable, and can be contrasted with the abstract 'system' – symbolised in distant neo-liberal university councils or government accountabilities – that is largely blamed for precarious employment or excessive research expectations. The neo-liberal university is unfriendly to everyone, but it is the academic community that needs to make space for difference.

The implications of this can be challenging to live with. As Ahmed (2010) suggests, some types of social justice require the capacity for people to live unhappily for significant periods and to embrace a shared discomfort that arises as communities adapt and engage in reform (see also Burford, 2017). But being uncomfortable is hard, tiring, painstaking and contributes to the sensation of being part of an unethical academy within an emotional logic that associates pleasure with the moral self. Some people actively distance themselves from such feeling, regarding it as too significant a burden (Ahmed, 2010). Notably, this can extend not only to critical issues of social inclusion, but to everyday responsibilities within academic communities. People wish to be part of the community but not to feel burdened, stressed, guilty, shamed or many of the other myriad of social feelings that act to mediate community life. They may even ask to be relieved of such emotional entanglements, given permission to be excused from the obligations that community entails, and so too to be excused from feeling 'bad' by such absence.

The working of this system can be seen in the debate around who should do peer reviewing – work largely done for free but necessary to maintaining research quality.[17] Doing your 'fair share' of this work is seen as an ethical obligation, but what is fair? Some suggest that you should do 2–3 times the number of papers you write (as each paper requires on average 2–3 reviewers), but peer review can be time-consuming and is largely unpaid. Thus, the burden of peer review should fall mainly on full-time, ideally tenured, academics, earning a good wage, who can fit it into their work schedule. Full-timers who have other responsibilities, like childcare, can reduce the number they do on those grounds. This of course leads to several problems: first, full-time, especially tenured, academics are now a minority in the academy (so this is an unrealistic request of the labour of this group); and, second, this action consolidates power over the production of knowledge with a minority. The point I am making here, however, is not just that this model of 'fairness' is impractical, but that such a solution quantifies an ethical commitment to a community, removes its emotional content and distributes that commitment across the body corporate according to a metrics of fairness. In this way, the 'guilt' associated with taking on this work is moderated – here is a benchmark that allows you to do 'enough' or to excuse yourself if you have a good enough reason, and your guilt can be adjusted according to your performance.

Discussions of community service within universities often focus on gender divisions, where women, not least minority women, are asked to perform the emotion work of pastoral care or university 'housework', especially in relation to inclusion. Men are often situated as oblivious to this labour, free of any guilt or shame about their failure to contribute (McFarlane and Burg, 2019; Heijstra et al., 2017). This, however, is somewhat different from the refusal of negative feeling seen here, where people recognise that a failure of duty should be discomforting, and so find ways to excuse themselves from the obligation. Academics are increasingly trained to do such refusals of feeling as a protective mechanism in an academy that asks too much. Thus, 'refusing to feel bad' about not working at the weekend – as is often expressed by academics – is both a commentary on the cruel discipline of university life and the

---

[17] See, for example, the discussion around Williams on Twitter, 13 May 2020, and McCann on Twitter, 5 May 2021.

possibility that we can distance ourselves from it (see the discussion around Guest on Twitter, 2 October 2021). At times, this can be seen as part of an ethics of refusal, where boundary-making is designed to enable other forms of social justice (such as providing opportunity for others). Yet, if this is the case, many in the academy become practised at distancing themselves from negative feeling and its associated obligations; choosing to live within such feeling as ethical practice is rarely considered outside of a small amount of feminist scholarship.

In all these accounts, negative feeling is figured as a form of work, that takes energy and resources from the human – a drain on the possibility of pleasure. Emotion is not simply a signifier of the operation of a larger system, but is itself managed to enable the ethical – happy – self to emerge. Managing bad feeling may even appear as a responsible action for the worker in readying themselves for the emotional demands of employment, saving energy for more productive purposes. In framing feeling as laborious, it can be placed alongside other work commitments and so allows for feeling to be a site of negotiation. The obligation of child-rearing that makes it difficult to attend an evening event can be used to justify and so offset any guilt about absence. This is often healthy and sensible, but it leads to ethical feeling being situated as a responsibility that competes with others, and which should primarily be taken up by those with time to do so. And here 'time' becomes associated with privilege, especially that held by the white, heterosexual man for whom the academy was made. In this way, personal responsibility within the academy is situated as a privilege, and privilege is imagined as time for action and, to a lesser extent, power.

A question that arises here is whether such a distribution of ethical commitment can enable a fairer academy, not least when it removes the 'passion' that academics place as central to the human. If the academic is imagined as an emotional actor whose feeling is a measure and performance of institutional morality, some forms of ethical feeling will be required of everyone if the academy is to meaningfully change to be more inclusive. Handing over that ethical responsibility to the privileged might acknowledge where the weight of power lies and the obligations that arise from such a positioning; but it also centres this group as the ethical heart of the academic community within a system where a refusal of such obligation is not only possible, but taught. Applying a logic of metricisation to our ethical commitments seems to risk producing the same discomforts and dehumanisation as it has in other areas of academic life. Rather, learning to live with some forms of discomfort as part of manifesting the ethical academic self might be as necessary to removing the suffering of academic life as the joys and pleasures of teaching and research. The challenge here is knowing what forms of suffering are a product of immoral behaviours or institutional cruelties, and which contribute to the production of an inclusive academy. Currently, however, such reflection is hampered by a model of the emotional self in which negative feeling has become too burdensome, within a system where the discomforts are already myriad.

## The Absent Norm

Many accounts of suffering highlight privilege as it adheres to particular bodies, or the ways that a raced and masculine norm still figures prominently as a disciplinary form within the university. Indeed, 'white men' are often situated as a symbol of the unethical institution, the group that need to change to reduce the suffering of others. These men can be real – there is not a shortage of 'bad' actors in the academy that can be pointed to – but as often they are symbolic of a refusal of care or ethical concern for the people that labour in the institution. In this way, 'white men' can be female, of a variety of ethnicities and can be the institution itself. The 'thanks for typing' meme is suggestive (Mazanec, 2017). Here, the many academic authors of the twentieth century that thanked anonymous wives for typing up their books are held up as evidence of the obliviousness of male privilege, where women performed unrewarded labour that advanced men's careers and men did not even provide the care of naming them in their acknowledgements. This relationship is considered exploitative, but it also a mirror of the behaviour of the largely male vice chancellors, senior managers and professors who have asked junior members of the academy to make unacknowledged sacrifices to allow its scale and success, while figuring such sacrifice as the entry fee required of those who wish to join its ranks (Pickwell, 2018). White men here become the embodiment of the wrongs of the academy.

This discourse has placed some restrictions on men in the academy. Accounts of male suffering, especially that of elite white men, are not always well received. Sometimes this is because individuals continue to show some of the obliviousness of the 'thanks for typing' meme. The men interviewed by Matthew Shepherd in his 1996 PhD complained about the strain of research expectations while simultaneously making their wives responsible for childcare, and failed to connect these gendered expectations to why women's success might be limited in the academy. As such, their complaints about 'strains' came across less as legitimate complaint, than as an unattractive lack of self-awareness. There is also a minority who believe that they are being isolated from their rightful place in the academy due to 'their' jobs going to 'undeserving' women and minorities, which most people agree is an illegitimate claim (Grasgreen, 2013). However, on many occasions, the inability of 'male' complaint to register with its audience is because the author fails to show appropriate recognition of their own privilege within a system of complaint in which the legitimacy of suffering is tied to structural positions of power.

Public complaint within the academy, as it appears in professional writings and on social media, requires a certain form; there are feeling rules that surround how, when and where it is appropriate to express particular forms of suffering. Juxtaposing different forms of grievance, especially when the complainants occupy structurally quite different positions within the hierarchy of university life, is viewed as inappropriate. Complaining about things that are only available to the privileged, without appropriate qualification and acknowledgement of a person's fortune, or criticising those with less structural power, tends to be viewed poorly. Rules of complaint come to act as a discipline on the privileged body that serves to remind them that the academy is an uncomfortable place and that feeling should be shared, until redress is brought to all within it. Those who fail to learn these rules – and they can require a nuance of form that can be challenging to master – can be disciplined to a greater or lesser extent. At its worst, this might extend to behaviours that the political right describes as 'cancel culture', such as Twitter mobbing, but more routinely involves disapproving remarks or comments on social media and online comment sections, or having your complaint ignored. The 'hurt feelings' of the powerful that might arise from these encounters are considered less significant than harms produced by the system which such individuals represent and sometimes enforce. The elite are asked to put their pain into proportion to that produced by the unethical practices of the institution, and from which they benefit.

This form of discipline is particularly exercised against those who produce narratives that are considered actively harmful to the 'soul' of the university. Here, the academy is imagined in terms of its vulnerable bodies and their sacrifices, and the professional choices or 'game-play' that individuals (often of necessity) engage in to succeed are rendered harms. Those who offer advice about how the system works, without at least an appropriate apologetics or acknowledgement of its problems, are read as enforcing the culture they describe, of allowing suffering to continue without scrutiny.[18] Those who defend such perspectives – sometimes viewing them as a harsh reality that there is little point complaining about or as part of the competitiveness that breeds institutional success – become part of the system that produces such harms. As a result, such contributions tend to be subject to particular disdain and only rarely defended, usually by those who think the author was perhaps a little careless in their choice of words – here, too, the defenders recognise there is a rhetorical form that should mediate such advice. Yet, if this is the case, undesirable attitudes and behaviours are more widely held than these often

---

[18] A great example of this phenomena can be explored by following responses to the tweet Boyer on Twitter, 30 June 2021.

more high-profile disputes suggest. Criticisms of tenured staff for not publishing enough, of retirees for not moving on, a naïve belief in the meritocracy of your place in the academy (and the just absence of those who never made it) and similar comments are common across all levels of the academy; they are often incorporated into complaint that is much more palatable to audiences, or where the lower structural position of the complainer discourages more senior members of the academy from adding to their suffering. Not all who hold others to account are without sin.

This creates a paradox in how academia as an institution operates as an emotional culture. On the one hand, power and privilege is vested in a small group, which we might refer to as 'white men', but, on the other, their emotions are remarkably absent in discussions of how an institution feels. There is, of course, a wider number of writings by senior academic men about how universities work, including several that address problems within the academy and the need for reform (Collini, 2012, 2017). Yet, the emotions of the elite rarely figure explicitly in such accounts. If they do emerge, it is often indirectly: the pride of the vice chancellor writing for other senior leaders of their successes, sometimes a delicately expressed exasperation that others do not see the value of their efforts (Johnson, 2020; Davis, 2017). An exception here might be the work on middle managers who are often regarded as similarly unhappy as others, often for the same reasons, but with a sense that the collegiality of those they manage is lacking (Heffernan and Bosetti, 2021). Here, the space for those without power to direct anger upwards leads to such managers being on the receiving end of complaint, which causes them upset. Like other academics, however, they rarely identify with 'the institution', so such pain is viewed as a form of suffering – one where unethical behaviour (like that identified by minorities) emerges from relationships with colleagues as well as the 'system'. Here and elsewhere, the emotions of the 'elite' are not rendered as distinctive from the general emotions of the academy. Thus, the emotional culture of the institution, as produced through the discourse of emotion in academic life, is one that arises from the affective community of the university, not its leaders, and where even its weakest members feature prominently in giving it shape.

This is suggestive of an emotional regime with a particular power and coherence across groups – academics are passionate and passion is manifested in emotional, authentic selves, where pleasure and pain operate as the measure of the ethics of the environment in which they are placed. Pain and suffering, expressed through complaint, signal the dysfunctions of the contemporary university and the need for reform. Those who deny such pain, or who fail to register it, are complicit in this suffering and, if they wish to participate in the academic public sphere, at least, can be disciplined into a discomfort that many experience as part of their daily lives. Here, a shared discomfort becomes a form of political solidarity. This can be refused or ignored – indeed, refusal of pain is critical to this emotional regime, where pain can be understood as ethical failing. If this is the case, happiness and joy – associated with teaching and research, the core mission of the institution – not only give hope, but suggest that academia still has a moral core and is worthy of reform.

## 7 Conclusion

The year 2020 was a watershed for anglophone academia, when the slow privatisation of universities, coupled with their massive expansion and disinvestment by the state, created an economic crisis when private incomes streams stuttered or looked imperilled as a consequence of COVID-19. In Australia, the result was a mass reduction in the workforce; a similar pattern appears to be emerging in the UK and the USA too. Following many years of contraction of academic jobs, and their replacement with shorter-term, casualised and less secure employment, the hope of the permanent position that had sustained many universities' precarious workers was significantly dented, if not entirely removed. Even the security of senior academics looks fragile, as universities seek to contract their workforces. The result is a considerable increase in expressions of dissatisfaction, sometimes tending towards political protest, across the academy.[19] This includes people at all academic levels and many who had not been especially politically engaged in the past.

Some in the academy were acutely politicised by these events, in a manner that might suggest a certain complacency, or sense that the academy was not previously especially cruel to them. Yet if that is the case, when mobilised, this group brought to their critique a shared understanding of the academy, its value and academic emotions as an ethical measure of the institution. Moreover, I would suggest that silence had not always reflected that this group had not shared in the discomforts of academic life (which, of course, varies across bodies), but that current conditions gave it a certain urgency, and perhaps a sense that this was a critical moment where something might change – hope arising from despair. If this is indeed the case, the anxieties and precarities of academic life have also taken on a new quality – fear is more palpable, and so the risk of doing nothing is also higher.

What does it mean to say that an institution feels? What does it mean to talk of the feelings of a group that is not only remarkably diverse but spread across different buildings, employers and countries? Rosenwein (2006) suggests that

---

[19] This can especially be seen in the number of people who have moved into union activities and protest organisations, as well as a greater degree of open complaint across social media.

an emotional community is one that shares a language and system of valuation for emotion. The academy with its agreed model of an emotional self, whose passion speaks to its freedom from institutional constraints, and its pains and pleasures that act to signify the ethics of the conditions in which it inhabits, can certainly be considered in those terms. To speak of institutional feeling, however, is suggestive of the group, of collective feeling that extends beyond the individual and their socialised emotional repertoire. Discourse here might matter. The institution is its texts – the way its members construct the whole through a shared emotional language – and the way that construction in textual form is also a performance of such feeling by individuals and by the group as they endorse, critique and entrain themselves through engagement in such cultural productions. The emotional culture of the institution, then, arises through these felt negotiations and expressions.

Here too we can see the politics of institutional feeling emerge and transform. Accounts of pain and pleasure, tied to particular experiences of institutional life (such as teaching or research or mobility across borders), give feeling and meaning to such experiences and, in doing so, locate them within an ethical system that falls along a pain–pleasure spectrum. This ethics acts as a commentary on the institution – an institution that is both the sum of its members, the behaviour of individuals within it and a wider amorphous 'system' located as beyond the control of the group. Thus, the feelings of the institution are a commentary on how the body operates as a whole, as well as the structures of power that act as a (sometimes coercive) discipline. Universities emerge as a disciplinary structure in which its attendant cruelties arise not only from a lack of care towards its members – although that is part of the story – but as we pursue participation in this affective community against 'the odds', against our own interests. In this, however, it is far from unique.

It is worth pausing here to address something that I have so far refused in this Element – the gap between the managerial class, who enforce the neo-liberal institution, and the academics who live within its system – the 'us and them'. My unwillingness to separate these groups is partly as both – in as much as we are academics (and not all are) – share the same emotional culture and use the same techniques to excuse our complicity, and its associated guilt, in a system that causes harm to individuals (Davis, Jansen van Rensburg and Venter, 2016). We all 'game-play' and engage with the system to ensure our position within it, however we may frame our apologetics for doing so; and we largely justify these decisions in relation to a greater good, whether that of the political project of our own research or the economic survival of a university whose income is driven by international student fees. Academics are also responsible for many of the tensions that have come to mark our experience of work – many of the systems used to measure research were (and still are) designed by academics for ourselves. The 'professional' opportunities that sit in tension with the vocational mission – whether grant writing workshops, books about writing productivity or mindfulness classes – are provided by academics as a support measure to help us succeed in this system: a literature of the passionate academic self, which gives our whole to the academy, is largely produced by us for us. The 'audit culture', with its systems of productivity and efficiency, may have been developed for business, but it was underpinned by academic research that promised the benefits of the 'scientific method' for the workplace – and for that reason shares a logic with much of our own scholarship about how to improve the world (Shore, 2015).

This is not to deny that external factors, including the implementation of new public management, have been influential in directing how universities function. Nor is it to deny that there are multiple emotional cultures within the university which some members have to negotiate; at least one of these is shaped by a more business-orientated pragmatism. But it is to suggest that we have played an important role in giving shape to the neo-liberal institution and that its form, including the contest around the nature of the academic self at its heart, has emerged as part of a conversation about what we wish to be – we place the boundary on how much engagement with the neo-liberal system is enough and discipline those who fail to show due discomfort when they cross it. While the dissonance we experience in the university is often blamed on the interference of an external system in our sense of vocation, we have been less willing to consider the ways that the vocation itself is also implicated in our suffering and how it has been produced as part of a dialectic with the 'professional'. We have given a lot more attention to describing and surviving the modern university than to its transformation. In this sense, the fractured self of the modern institution encapsulates that of its academic members.

The feeling institution as considered here is the profession/vocation, rather than particular universities. Different employers and the social, economic and political contexts in which they operate also influence how people experience working within the university. This matters: academics often share knowledge of working conditions and use that information strategically. Some employers are better at reducing some forms of suffering than others, or in enhancing opportunities for pleasure. If such conditions allow individuals to be more optimistic about what the academy is or can be, being part of the group nonetheless matters too. Others' suffering remains a concern – a threat to academic well-being. Within neo-liberal universities, where the pains seem to be growing exponentially, this threat can appear acute. If it has not impacted you yet, then it soon will. This is perhaps a particular challenge for managers of institutions that operate vocationally, where the decisions and actions made in response to local conditions come to be framed through a larger social, economic and political context, and the feeling cultures – including shared fears and anxieties – that are spread across the group. A shift in institutional culture requires attention not just to the emotional dynamics of a set of workers, but to the ways those workers are situated within a global network.

I began this Element with a reflection not on an emotional academic, but with a moment of absent feeling. The process of writing it has produced enough emotions of varying types to remind me that I am not as 'dispassionate' as I could perhaps wish. And yet, the current sufferings of the institution – the anxiety, fear and frustration about what the future holds for universities – have had a cooling effect (see, for example, Smith on Twitter, 30 April 2021 and replies). This might be especially true of the feelings of those who have chosen to leave academia entirely, but also in a rapidly growing scepticism towards claims about vocation, passion, and a greater good from universities that have shown little care for those who shape the self to their discipline. Such a cooling disrupts the ethic of an academy where passion is evidence of a free and authentic self, and its pains and pleasures operate as a guide to right and wrong. But it may be that such a cooling is necessary for reform, as we consider the harms that the vocational self demands of individuals in a precarious economy, and as we come to recognise that learning to sit in discomfort might be a necessary step in enabling us to work to be a more ethical academy. Avoiding 'bad feelings' might be less labour, but unjust nonetheless. The emotional self that is offered as the academy's self is not the only way to feel; as historians of emotion have demonstrated, emotions – how they are expressed, and their relationship to an ethical self – vary enormously across time and place. How they function to maintain and resist systems of power can change. As we consider how to reform the university to reduce the suffering of its majority, a more critical attention to the political work done by academic feeling is necessary.

# References

Adsit, J., Doe, S., Allison, M., Maggio, P. and Maisto, M. (2015). Affective activism: Answering institutional productions of precarity in the corporate university. *Feminist Formations*, 27(3), 21–48.

Ager, B. @BrittaAger (5 February 2021). Genuine question. . . Twitter Page. https://twitter.com/BrittaAger/status/1357520884538347522?s=20.

Ahmed, S. (2004). *The Cultural Politics of Emotion*, Edinburgh: Edinburgh University Press.

Ahmed, S. (2010). *The Promise of Happiness*, Durham, NC: Duke University Press.

Ahmed, S. (2012). *On Being Included: Racism and Diversity in Institutional Life*, Durham, NC: Duke University Press.

Ahmed, S. (2018). On complaint. *Wheeler Centre*. Available at: www.wheelercentre.com/broadcasts/sara-ahmed-on-complaint.

Ahmed, S. (2021). *Complaint*. Durham, NC: Duke University Press.

Ahoba-Sam, R. and Charles, D. (2019). Building of academics' networks – An analysis based on causation and effectuation theory. *Review of Regional Research*, 39, 143–61.

Archer, L. (2008a). Younger academics' constructions of 'authenticity', 'success' and professional identity. *Studies in Higher Education*, 33(4), 385–403.

Archer, L. (2008b). The new neoliberal subjects? Young/er academics' constructions of professional identity. *Journal of Education Policy*, 23(3), 265–85.

Arendt, H. (1958). *The Human Condition*, Chicago, IL: Chicago University Press.

Arnold-Forster, A. and Schotland, S. (2021). Covid-19 only exacerbated a longer pattern of health-care worker stress. *Washington Post*, 29 April. Available at: www.washingtonpost.com/outlook/2021/04/29/covid-19-only-exacerbated-longer-pattern-healthcare-worker-stress/.

Arvaja, M. (2017). Tensions and striving for coherence in an academic's professional identity work. *Teaching in Higher Education*, 23(3), 291–306.

Ashwin, P. (2015). Five ways universities have already changed in the 21$^{st}$ century. *The Conversation*, 14 May. Available at: https://theconversation.com/five-ways-universities-have-already-changed-in-the-21st-century-39676.

Askins, K. and Blazek, M. (2017). Feeling our way: Academia, emotions and a politics of care. *Social & Cultural Geography*, 18(8), 1086–1105.

Aswathi, M. @mnwsth (30 May 2021). A special round of thanks... Twitter Page. https://twitter.com/mnwsth/status/1398849517374492676?s=20.

Atay, A. (2017). Journey of errors: Finding home in academia. *Cultural Studies – Critical Methodologies*, 18(1), 16–22.

Atom44 (2020). Coping with survivor's guilt in academia. *Academia: StackExchange*. Available at: https://academia.stackexchange.com/ques tions/150909/coping-with-survivors-guilt-in-academia.

Attewell, N. (2016). Not the Asian you had in mind: Race, precarity, and academic labor. *English Language Notes*, 54(2), 183–90.

Baglini, R. and Parsons, C. (2020). If you can't be kind in peer review, be neutral. *Nature*, 30 November. Available at: www.nature.com/articles/ d41586-020-03394-y.

Barcan, R. (2016). *Academic Life and Labour in the New University: Hope and Other Choices*, London: Routledge.

Barcan, R. (2019). Weighing up futures: Experiences of giving up an academic career. In C. Manathunga and D. Bottrell, eds., *Resisting Neoliberalism in Higher Education Volume II: Prising Open the Cracks*, Cham: Springer International Publishing, pp. 43–64.

Barclay, K. (2019a). *Men on Trial: Performing Emotion, Embodiment and Identity in Ireland, 1800–1845*, Manchester: Manchester University Press.

Barclay, K. (2019b). Mobile emotions. *Historical Transactions*. Available at: https://blog.royalhistsoc.org/tag/katie-barclay/.

Barclay, K. (2021). *Caritas: Neighbourly Love and the Early Modern Self*, Oxford: Oxford University Press.

Barside, S. and Gibson, D. E. (2007). Why does affect matter in organizations? *Academy of Management Perspectives*, February, 36–59.

Barside, S. and O'Neill, O. A. (2016). Manage your emotional culture. *Harvard Business Review*, January–February. Available at: https://hbr.org/2016/01/ manage-your-emotional-culture.

Barton, N. @NimishaBarton (24 March 2021). Is there a word... Twitter Page. https://twitter.com/NimishaBarton/status/1374411048124440583?s=20.

Bartos, A. E. and Ives, S. (2019). Learning the rules of the game: Emotional labor and the gendered academic subject in the United States. *Gender, Place & Culture*, 26(6), 778–94.

Baty, P. @Phil_Baty (23 May 2021). 'Trailblazing' research agendas... Twitter Page. https://twitter.com/Phil_Baty/status/1396361951349985281?s=20.

Bellas, M. L. (1999). Emotional labor in academia: The case of professors. *American Academy of Political and Social Science*, 561, 96–110.

Bennett, D. Roberts, L. and Ananthram, S. (2017). Teaching-only roles could mark the end of your academic career. *The Conversation*, 28 March.

Available at: https://theconversation.com/teaching-only-roles-could-mark-the-end-of-your-academic-career-74826.

Berents, H. (2019). On academic precarity as ongoing anxiety. *Helen May Be Writing*, 19 February. Available at: https://helenmaybewriting.tumblr.com /post/182912719266/on-academic-precarity-as-ongoing-anxiety.

Berg, L. D., Huijbens, E. H. and Larsen, H. G. (2016). Producing anxiety in the neoliberal university. *The Canadian Geographer / Le Géographe Canadien*, 60(2), 168–80.

Berg, M. and Seeber, B. K. (2016). *The Slow Professor: Challenging the Culture of Speed in the Academy*, Toronto: University of Toronto Press.

Berlant, L. (2011). *Cruel Optimism*, Durham, NC: Duke University Press.

Berman, E. P. (2012). *Creating the Market University: How Academic Science Became an Economic Engine*, Princeton, NJ: Princeton University Press.

Bernier, J. W. @jwbernier (8 April 2021). When academics. . . Twitter Page. https://twitter.com/jwbernier/status/1379843878308708355?s=20.

Beudel, S. (2021). The exploitation of casual workers in the university sector. *Kill Your Darlings*, 8 February. Available at: www.killyourdarlings.com.au /article/the-exploitation-of-casual-workers-in-the-university-sector/.

Bijl, Mieke van der. (2020). Learning is joy – wellbeing challenges in pandemic higher education. *Mieke van der Bijl*, 20 June. Available at: https://medium .com/@miekevanderbijl/learning-is-joy-wellbeing-challenges-in-pandemic-higher-education-f74aaae67ec4.

Black, A. L. and Garvis, S., eds., (2018). *Lived Experiences of Women in Academia: Metaphors, Manifestos and Memoir*, London: Routledge.

Bloch, C. (2002). Managing the emotions of competition and recognition in academia. *The Sociological Review*, 50(2), 113–31.

Bloch, C. (2012). *Passion and Paranoia: Emotions and the Culture of Emotion in Academia*, Farnham, UK: Ashgate.

Bochner, A. P. (1997). It's about time: Narrative and the divided self. *Qualitative Inquiry*, 3(4), 418–38.

Boddice, R. @virbeatum (22 May 2021). I practice alienation. . . Twitter Page. https://twitter.com/virbeatum/status/1395836848061157388?s=20.

Bosanquet, A. (2018). Motherhood and academia: A story of bodily fluids and going with the flow. In A. L. Black and S. Garvis, eds., *Lived Experiences of Women in Academia: Metaphors, Manifestos and Memoir*, London: Routledge, pp. 65–75.

Boyer, D. @dominicboyer (30 June 2021). Elsevier sponsored 'rules of academia'. . . Twitter Page. https://twitter.com/dominicboyer/status/ 1398987182367383552?s=21.

Brennan, J. (2020). *Good Work If You Can Get It: How to Succeed in Academia*, Baltimore, MD: John Hopkins University Press.

Bright, D. (2017). The pleasure of writing: Escape from the dominant system. In S. Riddle, M. K. Harmes and P. A. Danaher, eds., *Producing Pleasure in the Contemporary University*, Rotterdam: Sense, pp. 37–48.

Britton, B. (2018). When hard work turns into academic obsession. *Editage Insights*, 12 November. Available at: www.editage.com/insights/passion-for-research-hard-work-or-academic-obsession?refer=scroll-to-1-article&refer-type=article-stories.

Broucker, B. and De Wit, K. (2015). New public management in higher education. In J. Huisman, H. de Boer, D. D. Dill and M. Souto-Otero, eds., *The Palgrave International Handbook of Higher Education Policy and Governance*, London: Palgrave Macmillan, pp. 57–75.

Brown, A. M. L. (2015). How not to be reviewer #2. *Ashley ML Brown*, Available at: https://amlbrown.com/2015/11/10/how-not-to-be-reviewer-2/.

Brown, N. and Leigh, J. (2018). Ableism in academia: Where are the disabled and ill academics? *Disability & Society*, 33(6), 985–9.

Brunila, K. and Valero, P. (2018). Anxiety and the making of research(ing) subjects in neoliberal academia. *Subjectivity*, 11(1), 74–89.

Bulaitis, Z. H. (2020). *Value and the Humanities: The Neoliberal University and Our Victorian Inheritance*, Cham: Palgrave Macmillan.

Burford, J. (2017). What might 'bad feelings' be good for? Some queer-feminist thoughts on academic activism. *Australian Universities Review*, 59(2), 70–8.

Burton, S. (2018). Writing yourself in? The price of playing the (feminist) game in the neoliberal university. In Y. Taylor and K. Lahad, eds., *Feeling Academic in the Neoliberal University: Feminist Flights, Fights and Failures*, Cham: Palgrave Macmillan, pp. 115–136.

Butler, N. and Spoelstra, S. (2020). Academics at play: Why the 'publication game' is more than a metaphor. *Management Learning*, 51(4), 414–30.

Cannizzo, F. (2018). 'You've got to love what you do': Academic labour in a culture of authenticity. *The Sociological Review,* 66(1), 91–106.

Cannizzo, F. and Osbaldiston, N., eds., (2019). *The Social Structures of Global Academia*, London: Routledge.

Cantor, G. (2020). The loneliness of the long-distance (PhD) researcher. *Psychodynamic Practice*, 26(1), 56–67.

Cantwell, B. and Kauppinen, I., eds., (2014). *Academic Capitalism in the Age of Globalization*, Baltimore, MD: John Hopkins University Press.

Carey, G. @gemcarey (22 April 2021). I was precarious. . . Twitter Page. https://twitter.com/gemcarey/status/1385044991156752384?s=20.

Carter, S., Guerin, C. and Aitchison, C. (2020). *Doctoral Writing: Practices, Processes and Pleasures*, Cham: Springer.

Caruso, J. (2021). Identity: Being Aboriginal in the academy: 'It's an identity thing'. In Adele Nye and Jennifer Clark, eds., *Teaching History for the Contemporary World: Tensions, Challenges and Classroom Experiences in Higher Education*, Cham: Springer, pp. 71–81.

Charteris, J., Gannon, S., Mayes, E., Nye, A. and Stephenson, L. (2016). The emotional knots of academicity: A collective biography of academic subjectivities and spaces. *Higher Education Research & Development*, 35(1), 31–44.

Chen, J. (2018). Coming to terms with six years in science: Obsession, isolation, and moments of wonder. *STAT*, 14 October, www.statnews.com/2018/10/14/phd-six-years-scientific-research/.

Chubb, J., Watermeyer, R. and Wakeling, P. (2017). Fear and loathing in the academy? The role of emotion in response to an impact agenda in the UK and Australia. *Higher Education Research & Development*, 36(3), 555–68.

Cohen, S., Hanna, P., Higham, J., Hopkins, D. and Orchiston, C. (2019). Gender discourses in academic mobility. *Gender, Work & Organization*, 27(2), 149-65.

Coin, F. (2018). When love becomes self-abuse: Gendered perspectives on unpaid labor in academia. In Y. Taylor and K. Lahad, eds., *Feeling Academic in the Neoliberal University: Feminist Flights, Fights and Failures*, Cham: Palgrave Macmillan, pp. 301–20.

Collini, S. (2012). *What Are Universities For?*, London: Penguin.

Collini, S. (2017). *Speaking of Universities*, London: Verso.

Collins, P. H. (2013). *Black Feminist Thought: Knowledge, Consciousness and the Politics of Empowerment*, 2nd ed., London: Routledge.

Commonwealth of Australia. (2018). Measuring the economic value of cultural and creative industries. Statistics Working Group of the Meeting of Cultural Ministers, Commonwealth of Australia.

Connell, R. (2019). *The Good University: What Universities Actually Do and Why It's Time For Radical Change*, London: Zed.

Crimmins, G. (2017). The intrinsic pleasure of being present with/in humanistic research. In S. Riddle, M. K. Harmes, and P. A. Danaher, eds., *Producing Pleasure in the Contemporary University*, Rotterdam: Sense, pp. 95–105.

Crimmins, G. (2018). The double life of a casual academic. In A. L. Black and S. Garvis, eds., *Lived Experiences of Women in Academia: Metaphors, Manifestos and Memoir*, London: Routledge, pp. 181–9.

Cruz, H. D. (2020). Dealing with the collapse in the academic job market: Advice for mentors and people on the job market. *The Philosophers' Cocoon*,

25 November. Available at: https://philosopherscocoon.typepad.com/blog/ 2020/11/dealing-with-the-collapse-in-the-academic-job-market-advice-for-mentors-and-people-on-the-job-market.html.

Currie, J., Thiele, B. and Harris, P. (2002). *Gendered Universities in Globalized Economies: Powers, Careers and Sacrifices*, Lanham, MD: Lexington Books.

David, M. E. (2016). *Feminism, Gender and Universities: Politics, Passion and Pedagogies*, London: Routledge.

Davis, A., Jansen van Rensburg, M. and Venter, P. (2016). The impact of managerialism on the strategy work of university middle managers. *Studies in Higher Education*, 41(8), 1480–94.

Davis, G. (2017). *The Australian Idea of the University*, Melbourne: Melbourne University Press.

Dear, L. (2019). The imperial/neoliberal university: What does it mean to be included?. In M. Breeze, Y. Taylor and C. Costa, eds., *Time and Space in the Neoliberal University: Future and Fractures in Higher Education*, Cham: Palgrave Macmillan, 93–118.

Decuir-Gunby, J. T. and Williams, M. R. (2007). The impact of race and racism on students' emotions: A critical analysis. In P. A. Schutz and R. Pekrun, eds., *Emotion in Education*, Cambridge: Elsevier, pp. 205–19.

Di Leo, J. R. (2006). Shame in academe: On the politics of emotion in academic culture. *JAC*, 26(1/2), 221–34.

Drążkiewicz, E. (2021). Blinded by the light: International precariat in academia. *Focaalblog*, 5 February, www.focaalblog.com/2021/02/05/ela-drazkiewicz-blinded-by-the-light-international-precariat-in-academia/.

Duffy, M. (2015). The hardest part of academia? Moving. *Dynamic Ecology*, 14 October. Available at: https://dynamicecology.wordpress.com/2015/10/ 14/the-hardest-part-of-academia-moving/.

Duncan, R., Tilbrook, K. and Krivokapic-Skoko, B. (2015). Does academic work make Australian academics happy? *Australian Universities Review*, 57 (1), 5–12.

Dunleavy, P. (2003). *Authoring a PhD: How to Plan, Draft, Write and Finish a Doctoral Thesis or Dissertation*, Basingstoke, UK: Palgrave Macmillan.

Duryea, E. D. and Williams, D. T. (2000). *The Academic Corporation: A History of College and University Governing Boards*, New York: Falmer Press.

Ehn, B., and Orvar L. (2007). Emotions in academia. In H. Wulff, ed., *The Emotions: A Cultural Reader*, Oxford: Berg Publishers, pp. 101–18.

Ehrenberg, R. G., eds., (2004). *Governing Academia*, Ithaca, NY: Cornell University Press.

Erickson, M., Walker. C. and Hanna, P. (2020). Survey of academics finds widespread feelings of stress and overwork. *The Conversation*, 29 February. Available at: https://theconversation.com/survey-of-academics-finds-widespread-feelings-of-stress-and-overwork-130715.

Evans, L. and Nixon, J., eds., (2015). *Academic Identities in Higher Education: The Changing European Landscape*, London: Bloomsbury.

Fabricant, M. and Brier, S. (2016). *Austerity Blues: Fighting for the Soul of Public Higher Education*, Baltimore, MD: John Hopkins University Press.

Fathi, R. and Megarrity, L. (2019). You matter: The Australian Historical Association's casualisation survey, Australian Historical Association. Available at: https://doi.org/10.25957/5e15063fb31a4.

Fem-Mentee Collective. (2017). Emotional masking and spill outs in the neo-liberalised university: A feminist geographic perspective on mentorship. *Journal of Geography in Higher Education*, 41(4), 590–607.

Female Science Professor. (2013). Happiness index. *Female Science Professor*, 4 April. Available at: http://science-professor.blogspot.com/2012/04/happiness-index.html.

Ferreira, V. K. (2017). Moving futures: Anthropological reflections on academic mobility and precarious life amongst South Asian social scientists in Europe. *Indian Anthropologist*, 47(1), 51–68.

Fetherston, C., Fetherston, A., Batt, S., Sully, M. and Wei, R. (2020). Wellbeing and work-life merge in Australian and UK academics. *Studies in Higher Education*. Available at: https://doi.org/10.1080/03075079.2020.1828326.

Firth, K., Connell, L. and Freestone, P. (2020). *Your PhD Survival Guide: Planning, Writing and Succeeding in Your Final Year*, London: Routledge.

Fitzmaurice, M. (2013). Constructing professional identity as a new academic: A moral endeavour. *Studies in Higher Education*, 38(4), 613–22.

Fitzpatrick, K. (2019). *Generous Thinking. A Radical Approach to Saving the University*, Baltimore. MD: John Hopkins University Press.

Flaherty, C. (2020). Barely getting by. *Inside Higher Ed*, 20 April. Available at: www.insidehighered.com/news/2020/04/20/new-report-says-many-adjuncts-make-less-3500-course-and-25000-year.

Forsyth, H. (2014). *A History of the Modern Australian University*, Sydney: NewSouth Publishing.

Foucault, M. (1988). Technologies of the Self. In L. H. Martin, H. Gutman and P. H. Hutton, eds., *Technologies of the Self: A Seminar with Michel Foucault*, Amherst, MA: The University of Massachusetts Press, pp. 16-49.

Frevert, U., Eitler, P. and Olsen, S. et al. (2014). *Learning How to Feel: Children's Literature and the History of Emotional Socialization, c. 1870–1970*, Oxford: Oxford University Press.

Game, A. and Metcalfe, A. (1996). *Passionate Sociology*, London: Sage.

Gannon, S. (2018). On being and becoming the monstrous subject of measurement. In S. Riddle, D. Bright, and E. Honan, eds., *Writing with Deleuze in the Academy: Creating Monsters*, Singapore: Springer, 73–93.

Gannon, S. and Gonick, G. (2019). Collective biography as a feminist methodology. In G. Crimmins, ed., *Strategies for Resisting Sexism in the Academy: Higher Education, Gender and Intersectionality.* Cham: Palgrave Macmillan, pp. 207–25.

Gannon, S. Taylor, C. and Adams, G. et al. (2019). 'Working on a rocky shore': Micro-moments of positive affect in academic work. *Emotion, Space and Society*, 31, 48–55.

Garrod, A., Kilkenny, R. and Benson Taylor, M., eds., (2017). *I Am Where I Come From: Native American College Students and Graduates Tell Their Life Stories*, Ithaca, NY: Cornell University Press.

Gill, R. (2009). Breaking the silence: The hidden injuries of the neoliberal university. In R. Ryan-Flood and R. Gill, eds., *Secrecy and Silence in the Research Process: Feminist Reflections*, London: Routledge, pp. 228–44.

Grasgreen, A. (2013). Majority disaffection. *Inside Higher Ed*, 22 March,. Available at: www.insidehighered.com/news/2013/03/22/white-men-alienated-higher-ed-workplace-survey-suggests.

Gregory, K. and Singh, S. S. (2018). Anger in academic twitter: Sharing, caring, and getting mad online. *TripleC: Communication, Capitalism & Critique. Open Access Journal for a Global Sustainable Information Society*, 16(1), 176–93.

Guest, O. @o_guest (2 October 2021). I'm an asst prof. Twitter Page. https://twitter.com/o_guest/status/1444013380591882247?s=20.

Haddow, G. and Hammarfelt, B. (2019). Early career academics and evaluative metrics: Ambivalence, resistance and strategies. In F. Cannizzo and N. Osbaldiston, eds., *The Social Structures of Global Academia*, London: Routledge, pp. 125–43.

Hall, R. (2018). *The Alienated Academic: The Struggle for Autonomy inside the University*, Basingstoke, UK: Palgrave Macmillan.

Hancox-Li, L. @struthious (13 April 2021). One very bad aspect. . . Twitter Page. https://twitter.com/struthious/status/1381785186594127872?s=20.

Harris, R. @racheldharris_ (19 May 2021). I honestly feel. . . Twitter Page. https://twitter.com/racheldharris_/status/1394778839985782786?s=20.

Hartung, C., Barnes, N. and Welch, R. et al. (2017). Beyond the academic precariat: A collective biography of poetic subjectivities in the neoliberal university. *Sport, Education and Society* 22(1), 40–57.

Hazelkorn, E. (2015). *Rankings and the Reshaping of Higher Education: The Battle for World-Class Education*, Basingstoke, UK: Palgrave Macmillan.

Heard, S. (2018). Academic nomads, academic settlers. *Scientist Sees Squirrel*. Available at https://scientistseessquirrel.wordpress.com/2018/02/15/academic-nomads-academic-settlers/.

Heffernan, T. and Bosetti, L. (2021). Incivility: the new type of bullying in higher education. *Cambridge Journal of Education*. Available at: https://doi.org/10.1080/0305764X.2021.1897524.

Heijstra, T. M., Einarsdóttir, þ. and Pétursdóttir, G. M. (2017). Testing the concept of academic housework in a European setting: Part of academic career-making or gendered barrier to the top? *European Educational Research Journal*, 16(2–3), 200–14.

Henderson, L., Honan, E. and Loch, S. (2016). The production of the academicwritingmachine. *Reconceptualizing Educational Research Methodology*, 7(2). Available at: https://doi.org/10.7577/rerm.1838.

Herzfeld, M. (1993). *The Social Production of Indifference*, Chicago, IL: Chicago University Press.

Hochschild, A. R. (2012). *The Managed Heart: Commercialization of Human Feeling*, Berkeley, CA: University of California Press.

Holeywell, K. (2009). The origins of a creative writing programme at the University of East Anglia, 1963–1966. *New Writing*, 6(1), 15–24.

Honan, E. (2017). Producing moments of pleasure within the confines of the neoliberal university. In S. Riddle, M. K. Harmes and P. A. Danaher, eds., *Producing Pleasure in the Contemporary University*, Rotterdam: Sense, pp. 13–24.

Horton, J. (2020). Failure failure failure failure failure failure: Six types of failure in the neoliberal academy. *Emotion, Space and Society*, 35. Available at: https://doi.org/10.1016/j.emospa.2020.100672.

Hrabowski, F. A., with Rous, P. J. and Henderson, P. H. (2019). *The Empowered University: Shared Leadership, Culture Change and Academic Success*, Baltimore, MD: John Hopkins University Press.

Huntington, S. @DrShaneRRR (21 May 2021). About 30% of. . . Twitter Page. https://twitter.com/DrShaneRRR/status/1395472525878956040?s=20.

Husemann, M., Rogers, R., Meyer, S. and Habel, J. C. (2017). 'Publicationism' and scientists' satisfactions depend on gender, career stage, and the wider academic system. *Palgrave Commun*, 3, 17032. Available at: https://doi.org/10.1057/palcomms.2017.32.

Ivancheva, M., Lynch, K. and Keating, K. (2019). Precarity, gender and care in the neoliberal academy. *Gender, Work & Organization*, 26(4), 448–62.

Jamie, K. (2020). Contesting the international mobility imperative in applications for academic promotion. *Conference Inference*, 6 April. Available at: https://conferenceinference.wordpress.com/2020/04/06/contesting-the-international-mobility-imperative-in-applications-for-academic-promotion-kimberly-jamie/.

Johnson, M. (2020). *Undermining Racial Justice: How One University Embraced Inclusion and Inequality*, Ithaca, NY: Cornell University.

Jones, D. R., Visser, M. and Stokes, P. et al. (2020). The performative university: 'targets', 'terror' and 'taking back freedom' in academia. *Management Learning*, 51(4). Available at: https://doi.org/10.1177/1350507620927554.

Josh is writing. @josh_iswriting (5 March 2021). I'm still reeling... Twitter Page. https://twitter.com/josh_iswriting/status/1367800877772378112?s=20.

Kara, H. (2017). Why I love reviewer 2. *Helen Kara*. Available at: https://helenkara.com/2017/07/18/why-i-love-reviewer-2/.

Kelsky, K. (2020). The academy is the grift. *The Professor Is In*, 14 September. Available at: https://theprofessorisin.com/2020/09/14/the-academy-is-the-grift/.

Kern, L., Hawkins, R., Falconer Al-Hindi, K. and Moss, P. (2014). A collective biography of joy in academic practice. *Social & Cultural Geography*, 15(7), 834–51.

Kernohan, D. (2019). A beginner's guide to academic workload modelling, *WONKHE*, 22 March. Available at: https://wonkhe.com/blogs/a-beginners-guide-to-academic-workload-modelling/.

Kezar, A., ed., (2011). *Recognizing and Serving Low-Income Students in Higher Education*, London: Routlege.

Kezar, A., DePaola, T. and Scott, D. T. (2019). *The Gig Academy: Mapping Labor in the Neoliberal University*, Baltimore, MD: John Hopkins University Press.

Khoo, T., Burford, J., Henderson, E., Liu, H. and Nicolazzo, Z. (2021). Not getting over it: The impact of Sara Ahmed's work within critical university studies. *Journal of Intercultural Studies*, 42(1), 84–98.

Kierkegaard, S. (2019/1846). *The Present Age: On the Death of Rebellion*, New York: Harper Perennial.

Lal, V. (2002). *Empire of Knowledge: Culture and Plurality in the Global Economy*, London: Pluto Press.

Lamont, M. (2009). *How Professors Think: Inside the Curious World of Academic Judgment*, Cambridge, MA: Harvard University Press.

Lau, J. (2021). 'Trailblazing' research agendas linked to academic mobility. *THE*, 23 May. Available at: www.timeshighereducation.com/news/trailblazing-research-agendas-linked-academic-mobility.

Leo, J. R. D. (2014). A dog's life: Austerity and conduct in neoliberal academe. *Symplokē*, 22(1–2), 59–76.

Lipton, B. (2017). The academic 'good life': Gender equality or cruel optimism? *Broad Agenda*, 16 July. Available at: www.broadagenda.com.au /2017/the-academic-good-life/.

Lipton, B. (2019a). Closed doors: Academic collegiality, isolation, competition and resistance in the contemporary Australian university. In M. Breeze, Y. Taylor and C. Costa, eds., *Time and Space in the Neoliberal University: Future and Fractures in Higher Education*, Cham: Palgrave Macmillan, pp. 15–43.

Lipton, B. (2019b). Academic anonymous: Blogging and feminist 'be/longings' in the neoliberal university. In A. Tsalapatanis, M. Bruce, D. Bissell and H. Keane, eds., *Social Beings, Future Belongings: Reimagining the Social*, London: Routledge, pp. 43–58.

Lister, K. @k8_lister (3 December 2019). I'm not saying... Twitter Page. https://twitter.com/k8_lister/status/1201760071455260672?s=20.

Liu, H. (2021). Workplace injury and the failing academic body: A testimony of pain. *Journal of Business Ethics*. Available at: https://doi.org/10.1007 /s10551-021-04838-9.

Lombardi, J. V. (2013). *How Universities Work*, Baltimore, MD: John Hopkins University Press.

Loughran, T. (2018). Blind spots and moments of estrangement: Subjectivity, class and education in British 'autobiographical histories'. In T. Loughran and D. Mannay, eds., *Emotion and the Researcher: Sites, Subjectivities, and Relationships: Studies in Qualitative Methodology*, Bingley, UK: Emerald, pp. 245–59.

Lund, R. and Tienari, J. (2019). Passion, care and eros in the gendered neoliberal university. *Organization*, 26(1), 98-121.

Lupton, D. (2013). The academic quantified self. *This Sociological Life*, 14 October. Available at: https://simplysociology.wordpress.com/2013/10/ 14/the-academic-quantified-self/.

Lupton, D. (2016). *The Quantified Self: A Sociology of Self-Tracking*, London: Wiley.

Luther, F. (2008). Publication ethics and scientific misconduct: The role of authors. *Journal of Orthodontics*, 35(1), 1-4.

Lutz, R. @rudilutz (8 May 2018). Oh the joys... Twitter Page. https://twitter .com/rudilutz/status/993793022793060352?s=20.

MacFarlane, B. and Burg, D. (2019). Women professors and the academic housework trap. *Journal of Higher Education Policy and Management*, 41 (3), 262–74.

Mackinlay, E. (2016). *Teaching and Learning Like a Feminist: Storying Our Experiences in Higher Education*, Rotterdam: Sense.

Manathunga, C., Selkrig, M., Sadler, K. and Keamy, R. K. (2017). Rendering the paradoxes and pleasures of academic life: Using images, poetry and drama to speak back to the measured university. *Higher Education Research & Development*, 36(3), 526–40.

Mandler, P. (2020). *The Crisis of the Meritocracy: Britain's Transition to Mass Education since the Second World War*, Oxford: Oxford University Press.

Manzi, M., Ojeda, D. and Hawkins, R. (2019). 'Enough wandering around!': Life trajectories, mobility, and place making in neoliberal academia. *The Professional Geographer*, 71(2), 355–63.

Marinetto, M. (2020). Who put the cult in faculty? *THE*, 1 January. Available at: www.timeshighereducation.com/opinion/who-put-cult-faculty.

Matthew, P. A., ed., (2016). *Written/Unwritten: Diversity and the Hidden Truths of Tenure*, Chapel Hill, NC: University of North Carolina Press.

Mazanec, C. (2017). #thanksfortyping spotlights unnamed women in literary acknowledgements. *NPR*, 30 March. Available at: www.npr.org/2017/03/30/521931310/-thanksfortyping-spotlights-unnamed-women-in-literary-acknowledgements.

McCann, H. @binarythis (5 May 2021). Given every article... Twitter Page. https://twitter.com/binarythis/status/1389764948918620162?s=20.

McKenzie, L. (2017). A precarious passion: Gendered and age-based insecurity among aspiring academics in Australia. In R. Thwaites and A. Pressland, eds., *Being an Early Career Feminist Academic: Global Perspectives, Experiences and Challenges*, London: Palgrave Macmillan, pp. 31–49.

McKenzie, L. (2019). Invisible anger: Intergenerational dependence and resentment among precarious academics. In J. M. Puaschunder, ed., *Intergenerational Responsibility in the 21st Century*, Wilmington, DE: Vernon Press, pp. 33–54.

McMillan, B. (2016). Think like an imposter, and you'll go far in academia. *THE*, 18 April. Available at: www.timeshighereducation.com/blog/think-impostor-and-youll-go-far-academia.

Melby-Lervåg, M. @lervag (4 December 2020). So tired of... Twitter Page. https://twitter.com/lervag/status/1334560808139956224?s=20.

Mewburn, I. and Thomson, P. (2018). Towards an academic self? Blogging during the PhD. In D. Lupton, I. Mewburn and P. Thomson, eds., *The Digital Academic: Critical Perspectives on Digital Technologies in Higher Education*, London: Routledge, pp. 20–35.

Michell, D., Wilson, J. and Archer, V., eds., (2015). *Bread and Roses: Voices of Australian Academics from the Working Class*, Leiden: Brill.

Minnix, C. (2018). *Rhetoric and the Global Turn in Higher Education*, Cham: Palgrave Macmillan.

Mittermeier, S. @ S_Mittermeier (6 March 2021). I am not asking... Twitter Page. https://twitter.com/S_Mittermeier/status/1367875572802727938?s=20.

Moisander, J. K., Hirsto, H. and Fahy, K. M. (2016). Emotions in institutional work: A discursive perspective. *Organization Studies*, 37(7), 963–90.

Moreton-Robertson, A. (2004). Whiteness, epistemology and indigenous representation. In Aileen Moreton-Robinson, ed., *Whitening Race: Essays in Social and Cultural Criticism*, Canberra: Australian Studies Press, pp. 75–88.

Morrish, L. (2019). Pressure vessels: The epidemic of poor mental health among higher education staff. HEPI Occasional Paper 20. Available at: www.hepi.ac.uk/2019/05/23/pressure-vessels-the-epidemic-of-poor-mental-health-among-higher-education-staff/.

Moss, P., Kern, L. Hawkins, R. and Falconer Al-Hindi, K. (2018). Grasping the affirmative: Power and the process of becoming joyful academic subjects. *Emotion, Space and Society*, 28, 53–59.

Moss, R. (2019). A memoir in blood; or a history of grace. *Rachel E. Moss*, 19 June. Available at: https://rachelemoss.com/2019/06/19/a-memoir-in-blood-or-a-history-of-grace/.

Moss, R. (2020). Precarity has a long hangover. *THE*, 12 February. Available at: www.timeshighereducation.com/opinion/precarity-has-long-hangover.

Myers, D. G. (1993). The rise of creative writing. *Journal of the History of Ideas*, 54(2), 277–97.

Nakata, M. (2007). *Disciplining the Savages, Savaging the Disciplines*, Canberra: Aboriginal Studies Press.

Niesche, R. and Haase, M. (2012). Emotions and ethics: A Foucauldian framework for becoming an ethical educator. *Educational Philosophy and Theory*, 44(3), 276–88.

O'Grady, C. (2021). Academia is often a family business. That's a barrier for increasing diversity. *Science*, 1 April. Available at: www.sciencemag.org/careers/2021/04/academia-often-family-business-s-barrier-increasing-diversity.

O'Neill, M. (2014). The slow university: Work, time and well-being. *Forum: Qualitative Social Research*, 15(3). Available at: www.qualitative-research.net/index.php/fqs/article/view/2226/3696.

O'Shea, T. @DrTomOShea (28 April 2021). Class has shaped... Twitter Page. https://twitter.com/DrTomOShea/status/1387389694191837187?s=20.

Oakley, C. (2010). Dr Amanda Barnard, computational physicist. *Australian Academy of Science*. Available at: www.science.org.au/learning/general-audi

ence/history/interviews-australian-scientists/dr-amanda-barnard-computational.

OECD. (2012). *Transferable Skills Training for Researchers Supporting Career Development and Research: Supporting Career Development and Research*, Paris: OECD Publishing.

Orr, Y. and Orr, R. (2016). The death of Socrates: Managerialism, metrics and bureaucratisation in universities. *Australian Universities Review*, 58(2), 15–25.

Ortolano, M. (2020). Is relocating necessary in academia? *Academic Stack Exchange*. Available at: https://academia.stackexchange.com/questions/149759/is-relocating-necessary-in-academia.

Osbaldiston, N., Cannizzo, F. and Mauri, C. (2019). 'I love my work but I hate my job' – Early career academic perspective on academic times in Australia. *Time & Society*, 28(2), 743–62.

Patton, S. (2012). Stale PhD's need not apply. *Chronicle of Higher Education*, 19 September. Available at: www.chronicle.com/article/stale-ph-d-s-need-not-apply/.

Pelch, M. (2018). Gendered differences in academic emotions and their implications for student success in STEM. *International Journal of STEM Education*, 5(33). Available at: https://doi.org/10.1186/s40594-018-0130-7.

Pereira, M. D. M. (2017). *Power, Knowledge and Feminist Scholarship: An Ethnology of Academia*, London: Routledge.

Perera, S. @DrSudaPerera (5 June 2020). My contract… Twitter Page. https://twitter.com/DrSudaPerera/status/1268843641663115264?s=20.

Perraton, H. (2014). *A History of Foreign Students in Britain*, Basingstoke, UK: Palgrave Macmillan.

Peseta, T., Barrie, S. and McLean, J. (2017). Academic life in the measured university: Pleasures, paradoxes and politics. *Higher Education Research & Development*, 36(3), 453–7.

Phan, L. H. and Childs, K. (2017). *Student Surveys of Teaching & Learning Quality*, Brisbane: University of Queensland.

Pickwell, J. (2018). Scientists reveal their sacrifices for the sake of work. *Nature Index*, 21 May. Available at: www.natureindex.com/news-blog/scientists-reveal-the-sacrifices-made-for-the-sake-of-work.

Pine, E. (2018) *Notes to Self*, London: Penguin.

Posick, C. (2018). Academia is stressful. Mindfulness tips for academics. *Psychreg*, 22 December. Available at: www.psychreg.org/mindfulness-academics/.

Potter, T. (2021), Competence is underrated. *Small Pond Science*, 29 April. Available at: https://smallpondscience.com/2021/04/29/competence-is-underrated/.

Rafaeli, A. and Worline, M. (2001). Individual emotion in work organization. *Social Science Information*, 40(1), 95–123.

Rawat, S. and Meena, S. (2014). Publish or perish: Where are we heading? *Journal of Research in Medical Sciences*, 19(2), 87–9.

Reale, E., Bleiklie, I. and Ferlie, E., eds., (2009). *University Governance: Western European Comparative Perspectives*, Cham: Springer.

Reddy, W. (2001). *The Navigation of Feeling: A Framework for the History of Emotions*, Cambridge: Cambridge University Press.

Rees, Y. @YvesRee (21 May 2021). I've been reflecting... Twitter Page. https://twitter.com/YvesRees/status/1395602845483765768?s=20.

Reiter, J. (2015). The joy of archival research. *English Historical Fiction Authors*, 4 March. Available at: https://englishhistoryauthors.blogspot.com /2015/03/the-joy-of-archival-research.html.

Riddle, S., Harmes, M. K. and Danaher, P. A., eds., (2017). *Producing Pleasure in the Contemporary University*, Rotterdam: Sense.

Roberts-Miller, T. (2014). 9-5. *Inside Higher Ed*, 25 August. Available at: www .insidehighered.com/advice/2014/08/25/essay-working-40-hours-week-academic.

Rogers, N. (2016). Specialised grants allow scientists to restart careers. *Spectrum*, 14 November. Available at: www.spectrumnews.org/news/special ized-grants-allow-ex-scientists-restart-careers/.

Rosenwein, B. (2006). *Emotional Communities in the Early Middle Ages*, Ithaca, NY: Cornell University Press.

Rosenwein, B. (2015). *Generations of Feeling: A History of Emotions*, Cambridge: Cambridge University Press.

Ross, J. (2021). Excessive selection criteria bogging down academic recruitment. *THE*, 22 January. Available at: www.timeshighereducation.com/news/ excessive-selection-criteria-bogging-down-academic-recruitment.

Ruben, A. (2012). Does scientific research needs a purpose? *Science*, 23 November. Available at: www.sciencemag.org/careers/2012/11/does-scientific-research-need-purpose.

Sadler, K., Selkrig, M. and Manathunga, C. (2017). Teaching is . . . opening up spaces to explore academic work in fluid and volatile times. *Higher Education Research & Development*, 36(1), 171–86.

Salas, M. (2018). The emotion of discovery is a profound and incomparable feeling. *UABDivulga*, 30 April. Available at:www.uab.cat/web/news-detail/ the-emotion-of-discovery-is-a-profound-and-incomparable-feeling-1345680342044.html?noticiaid=1345755834542.

Salminen-Karlsson, M., Wolffram, A. and Almgren, N. (2018). Excellence, masculinity and work-life balance in academia: Voices from researchers in

Germany and Sweden. *International Journal of Gender, Science and Technology*, 10(1), 53–71.

Salt, D. (2002). Dr Rohan Baker, molecular geneticist. *Australian Academy of Science*. Available at:www.science.org.au/learning/general-audience/history/interviews-australian-scientists/dr-rohan-baker-molecular#8.

Saunders, M. (2018). Moving for academic careers is not 'just like other jobs'. *Ecology Is Not a Dirty Word*, 19 February. Available at: https://ecologyisnotadirtyword.com/2018/02/19/moving-for-academic-careers-is-not-just-like-other-jobs/.

Scheer, M. (2012). Are emotions a kind of practice (and is that what makes them have a history)? A Bordieuian approach to understanding emotion. *History and Theory*, 51(2), 193–220.

Schepelern Johansen, B. (2020). Secular excitement and academic practice. In C. Von Scheve, A. L. Berg, M. Haken and N. Y. Ural, eds., *Affect and Emotion in Multi-Religious Secular Societies*, London: Routledge, pp. 195–210.

Schuster, J. H. and Finkelstein, M. J. (2006). *The American Faculty: the Restructuring of Academic Work and Careers*, Baltimore. MD: John Hopkins University Press.

Scully, M. @marcdonnchadh (3 June 2021). I've seen this flowchart. Twitter Page. https://twitter.com/marcdonnchadh/status/1400433680615620608?s=20.

Shepherd, M. (1996). Re-thinking masculinity: Discourses of gender and power in two workplaces. PhD thesis, University of Sheffield.

Shepherd, S. (2017). Managerialism: An ideal type. *Studies in Higher Education*, 43(9), 1668–78.

Shepperd, J. @joshshepperd (1 April 2021). This generation... Twitter Page. https://twitter.com/joshshepperd/status/1377292609165488132?s=20.

Shore, C. and Wright, S. (2015). Audit culture revisited: Rankings, ratings and the reassembling of society. *Current Anthropology*, 56(3), 421–44.

Showalter, E. (2005). *Faculty Towers: The Academic Novel and Its Discontents*, Oxford: Oxford University Press.

Shreve, G. (2018). 'Quit lit' then and now. *Inside Higher Ed*, 4 April. Available at: www.insidehighered.com/views/2018/04/04/comparison-quit-lit-1970s-and-today-opinion.

Singh, N. @naunihalpublic (10 March 2021). For my academic friends... Twitter Page. https://twitter.com/naunihalpublic/status/1369313863070519296?s=20.

Sinykin, D. (2016). Intellect, endoscopy. *Avidly: with Intense Eagerness*, 5 January. Available at: http://avidly.lareviewofbooks.org/2016/01/05/intellect-endoscopy/.

Smith, C. A. (2021). 'We are not named': Black women and the politics of citation in Anthropology. *Feminist Anthropology*, 2(1), 18–37.

Smith, K. and Bandola-Gill, J. (2020). *The Impact Agenda: Controversies, Consequences and Challenges*, Bristol: Polity Press.

Smith, K. M. @drkyliesmith (30 April 2021). What is the point. . . Twitter Page. https://twitter.com/drkyliesmith/status/1387819654429777933?s=20.

Snackowski, C. @carometonym (21 May 2021). Academia's professionalized feelings. . . Twitter Page. https://twitter.com/carometonym/status/1395521130887327747?s=20.

Sullenwizard. (2021). Do you ever feel like your research is pointless? *Reddit Ask Academia*. Available at: www.reddit.com/r/AskAcademia/comments/ca3il1/do_you_ever_feel_like_your_research_is_pointless/.

Summerville, A. @RegretLab (24 April 2021). Why am I glad. . . Twitter Page. https://twitter.com/RegretLab/status/1385622529361039367?s=20.

Taylor, B. (2020). Working in science was a brutal education. That's why I left. *BuzzFeed News*, 17 February. Available at: www.buzzfeednews.com/article/brandontaylor/i-dont-miss-being-a-scientist-except-when-i-do.

Taylor, Y. and Lahad, K., eds., (2018). *Feeling Academic in the Neoliberal University: Feminist Flights, Fights and Failures*, Cham: Palgrave Macmillan.

Teelken, C., Taminiau, Y. and Rosenmöller, C. (2021). Career mobility from associate to full professor in academia: Micro-political practices and implicit gender stereotypes. *Studies in Higher Education*, 46(4), 836–50. Available at: https://doi.org/10.1080/03075079.2019.1655725.

Thouaille, M.-A. (2018). Is pursuing an academic career a form of 'cruel optimism'? *LSE Blog*, 1 March. Available at: https://blogs.lse.ac.uk/impactofsocialsciences/2018/03/01/is-pursuing-an-academic-career-a-form-of-cruel-optimism/.

Tolley, K., ed., (2018). *Professors in the Gig Economy: Unionizing Adjunct Faculty in America*. Baltimore, MD: John Hopkins University Press.

Torralba, J. M. (2020). 10 rules to survive in the marvellous but sinuous world of academia. *Elsevier Connect*, 17 April. Available at: www.elsevier.com/connect/10-rules-to-survive-in-the-marvellous-but-sinuous-world-of-academia.

Tuhiwai Smith, L. (2013). *Decolonizing Methodologies: Research and Indigenous Peoples*, London: Zed Books.

u/smaller_bear. (2020). For us average people in academia: When in your academic career did you realize that you weren't going to be a star and what prompted it? *Reddit*. Available at: www.reddit.com/r/AskAcademia/comments/hzi3x1/for_us_average_people_in_academia_when_in_your/.

Vatansever, A. (2020). *At the Margins of Academia: Exile, Precariousness and Subjectivity*, Leiden: Brill.

Vila, A. C. (2018). *Suffering Scholars: Pathologies of the Intellectual in Enlightenment France*, Philadelphia, PA: University of Pennsylvania Press.

Wayne, L. and Yao, C. (2016). The trap of overachievement. *PhDivas*, season 2, episode 3. Available at: https://soundcloud.com/phdivas/trap-of-overachievement.

Weber, M. (1919). *Wiessenchaft als Beruf*, Munich: Duncker & Humblodt.

Williams, P. @DrPaulDWilliams (13 May 2020). I am getting. . . Twitter Page. https://twitter.com/DrPaulDWilliams/status/1257386074164396033?s=20.

Wilsdon, J. (2015). In defence of the research excellence framework. *The Guardian*, 28 July. Available at: www.theguardian.com/science/political-science/2015/jul/27/in-defence-of-the-ref.

Wogrammer. (2012). Is 9 to 5 possible for a woman in academia? *Life as a Professor*, 14 February. Available at: https://medium.com/wogrammer/life-as-a-professor-877542b97841.

Wolfe, M. J. and Mayes, E. (2019). Response-ability: Re-e-valuing shameful measuring processes within the Australian academy. In M. Breeze, Y. Taylor and C. Costa, eds., *Time and Space in the Neoliberal University: Future and Fractures in Higher Education*, Cham: Palgrave Macmillan, pp. 277–97.

Ylijoki, O.-H. (2020). Happy in academia: The perspective of the academic elite. In F. Cannizzo and N. Osbaldiston, eds., *The Social Structures of Global Academia*, London: Routledge, pp. 107–22.

Zembylas, M. (2007). A politics of passion in education: The Foucauldian legacy. *Educational Philosophy and Theory*, 39(2), 135–49.

Zembylas, M. and Schutz, P. A., eds., (2016). *Methodological Advances in Research on Emotion and Education*, Cham: Springer.

Cambridge Elements ≡

# Histories of Emotions and the Senses

## Jan Plamper

*University of Limerick*

Jan Plamper is Professor of History at the University of Limerick. His publications include *The History of Emotions: An Introduction* (Oxford, 2015); a multidisciplinary volume on fear; and articles on the sensory history of the Russian Revolution and on the history of soldiers' fears in World War One. He has also authored *The Stalin Cult: A Study in the Alchemy of Power* (Yale, 2012) and *Das neue Wir: Warum Migration dazugehört. Eine andere Geschichte der Deutschen* (S. Fischer, 2019).

## About the Series

Born of the emotional and sensory 'turns', *Elements in Histories of Emotions and the Senses* move one of the fastest-growing interdisciplinary fields forward. The series is aimed at scholars across the humanities, social sciences, and life sciences, embracing insights from a diverse range of disciplines, from neuroscience to art history and economics. Chronologically and regionally broad, encompassing global, transnational, and deep history, it concerns such topics as affect theory, intersensoriality, embodiment, human-animal relations, and distributed cognition.

Cambridge Elements ≡

# Histories of Emotions and the Senses

## Elements in the Series

A full series listing is available at: www.cambridge.org/EHES

Printed in the United States
by Baker & Taylor Publisher Services